Playing Project Manager

CHARLES SMITH

Copyright © Charles Smith 2014

CopyrightDeposit.com number 0031632

All rights reserved.

ISBN: 1502444968
ISBN-13: 978-1502444967

Cover photo: floor at Tabley House, Knutsford

CONTENTS

	Preface	vii
	Acknowledgments	xi
1	Project Managers as Performers	1
2	Being a Project Manager	11
3	Getting Hold of the Plot	25
4	Playing the Analyst	39
5	Playing the Enforcer	51
6	Playing the Expert	67
7	Playing the Impresario	79
8	Playing the Master of Ceremonies	91
9	Playing the Reshaper	101
10	Project Lives: Archetypes and Careers	113
	Appendix: Notes on Research and Literature	127
	Bibliography	132

PREFACE

This book is about project managers, and the matter of how one speaks and acts to become, and establish oneself as, a manager in the world of projects. It is founded upon stories, and the proposition that the stories people tell reveal who they are. In this preface I introduce the book by way of telling my own story (and hence perhaps revealing something of myself) about how it came to be written.

The origins of the book lie some 20 years ago. The industry I worked in suffered a severe downturn, and the company where I was employed had to reduce its numbers sharply and change its way of doing business. From being a middle manager in an engineering discipline where I had fair degree of knowledge, I suddenly became the manager responsible for a range of initiatives – we tried most of the management fads of the day – aimed at transforming the company.

We had some success (the company survived). However throughout this period I was uneasy in that I had no coherent approach to understanding how people thought and acted at work. I decided, perhaps like an engineer, that I wanted to go back to some basic principles, and I started to take an interest in psychology, enrolling for an Open University degree in that subject. The degree covered much material, but I found I was particularly drawn to constructivist styles of thinking: the various perspectives in psychology on how people individually and collectively make sense of themselves and their world. This style of thinking permeates the present book.

The fact that my interest is now specifically concerned with project managers is largely serendipitous. With the degree attained I started to cast around for a new opportunity. This turned out to be a position as manager of a project in financial services, bringing in new management structures, practices and IT systems, and drastically reducing staff numbers. At this point I knew nothing of financial services, and moreover I had never been a project manager, although I had worked for years on major construction projects, and project practices had been a big concern in the organisation changes I had dealt with. The project of my new appointment was highly technical, and highly political.

After two years the project was complete (good enough to go into operation) and I was a free agent. I was keen to write. I had been doing a lot of reading on psychology, and talking with others, and wanted to connect my thinking to my experiences as a manager. I wrote a reflective paper on this topic, and dared to present it at an academic workshop.

This act bought me into the realm of project management academia. I was appointed coordinator for an international research network, which drew me into organising academics, and contributing to papers that pulled together the thinking emerging from the meetings of the research network. (The academics were remarkably supportive to me, on occasion referring to me as a quasi-academic.)

When the research network had reached its conclusions, and published its papers, I wrote my own book on the subject, *Making Sense of Project Realities*. (This is less than half of a very long title. From here on I shall refer to it as *MSPR*.) This book was largely informed by the work of the network, but supplemented from my own experience. It describes projects and their management from my preferred perspective – as socially constructed entities, driven by political forces and the personal volition of individuals who have highly factional interests.

Initially I thought that was the end of the matter, but slowly I became aware that I had unfinished business, which was to return to my original concern to find a coherent way of understanding how people think and act at work. Real people had appeared in *MSPR*, and indeed the central creed of the research network had been to base its investigations on realities as told by practitioners. However the fundamental focus of *MSPR* is on the 'object' – the project. People appear as informants on the nature of projects. The nature of the people themselves, however, is covered only briefly. I wanted to reverse the telescope, to find a way to examine the subjects, the people who were speaking, and take a more thorough look at how they think and act – their identities as project managers.

Believing that enlightenment could only be found through researching the lived experiences of project managers, I gained permission to examine dissertations of post-graduate students, which included reflections on their experiences as managers. Using the dissertations as examples, I devised a methodology for studying identities, based on collecting and analysing stories from managers. I published a paper on this methodology in the academic press (with valuable support from my academic friends). The paper was subject to peer review, which was difficult, but the reviewers made no criticism of my approach, so I set off.

Using a very simple research question ("Tell me about a project challenge and how you handled it.") I collected stories, initially by pestering friends and relatives, then moving on to petition a wider population of managers via social media.

The outcome of my analysis, the nature of the identities of the project managers who tell these stories, is presented in this book. My intent has been to make this readable for a general audience of managers, and to this end the literature on the subject has not been presented or discussed in the text. The topic of my book is the lives of managers. I want my observations to emerge from the thinking of those managers, and to stand on their contributions, rather than on an enquiry into what other authorities have had to say. Apart from the words of active project managers, the only people I have cited in the text are Niccolo Machiavelli (1469–1527), Ben Jonson (1572–1637), and the Holy Roman Emperor, Charles V (1500–1558).

That said however my mode of investigation and my analysis have been massively influenced by many others, and so I have summarised relevant literature, and its connection to my work, in an appendix.

The adoption of project managers as my field of study has, I think, been fortuitous. They are a broad but definable group of people, and they have been open and enthusiastic storytellers. I have enjoyed working with them. I hope they will find the outcome of my endeavours of value, to their aspirations and to their careers as managers.

Charles Smith, Knutsford

October 2014

ACKNOWLEDGMENTS

This book is founded on the stories told to me by practising managers. Without them there would be no book. They include Edwin Chia, Max Cooke, John Fisher, Jon Hyde, Lisa Johnson, Chris Ivory, Oliver Jones, Dan Kushner, Taralyn Frasqueri-Molina, Franklin Riley, Hala Saleh, Nirmal Singh, Peter Southcombe and Howard Thompson. Others prefer not to be named.

Concerning my research, Mark Winter at Manchester Business School has encouraged me and acted as a sympathetic critic. I have also benefited greatly from many discussions in York with members of Helen Jones's psychology research group.

In writing the book itself, I have been supported throughout by the encouragement my wife Helen, who has also cast her editorial eye over my writings.

To all these people, I offer my sincere thanks.

1. PROJECT MANAGERS AS PERFORMERS

On the project stage

There are good pragmatic reasons why people engaged in the management of projects should think of themselves as performers, and the world of projects as the stage on which they play their roles. It is through their performances that managers establish their reputations. Their credibility is built not on their knowledge of mechanised practices and administrative procedures, but on how they handle the complexities and challenges of the real project world.

By studying the performances of real managers, as they deal with real project situations, we can learn about their identities: the people they must be, or become, if they are to act effectively. We can categorise and describe the identities that managers adopt, and so provide guidance to those making their way in the profession. They will be able to ask themselves "could I do that?" or perhaps "would I want to?" We can discover the strengths and strategies a person needs to perform the role in a particular way.

To understand project management in terms of personal performances we need to establish some principles about the nature of individual action in the social world, applying these principles to managers in the world of projects. To this end we shall start by looking at a short example, a story related by Paul:

> *I was asked to attend, and chair, a project review meeting on the delivery of a major software and hardware update to [...], which had a poor history of problems and a negative reputation, in place of my boss who couldn't attend. ...*
>
> *When I attended the meeting it lasted a couple of hours and appeared more a bun fight with all the sub-contractors blaming the prime contractor, and was a fairly chaotic session. The overall project also had a complex hierarchy with multiple levels of management control due to the nature of the contract.* [NB Explanatory diagrams and charts are attached to Paul's original story text.]
>
> *After this meeting, I took over the project and it became one of my responsibilities to manage it to a successful conclusion. This meant I then attended the Quarterly Customer meeting, which followed a very similar pattern to the project review, except all the customers joined the sub-contractors and also blamed the prime contractor! And it lasted a full day!*
>
> *When the time came for the next project review meeting I decided to hold it the day before the Quarterly Customer meeting. At the end of the meeting (at the start of any other business) I emphasised the fact that we needed to present a united front in order to be seen as credible suppliers (I used the metaphor of "not washing our dirty linen in public") and then laid down some ground rules for the next day. These were:*
>
> - *I would lead all the discussions and answer for us all.*
> - *I would invite other members of our team to talk to answer questions in their specialist area.*
> - *Nothing was to be discussed that we hadn't discussed, and agreed a solution to, in our meeting.*
>
> *I then went round the table asking everyone for anything else they wanted me to bring up, or they thought might be covered, the next day.*
>
> *At the meeting next day I sat directly opposite the Chair and*

took control of our responses. As the meeting was coming to an end, a question was asked of the equipment manufacturer which had not been covered the day before. To his credit the manufacturer looked at me, apologised and asked permission to answer – which I gave, adding "this time".

This is quite a performance! In many ways Paul's story might be seen as a traditional project management fable. A situation of chaos is to be transformed into a realm of order. Paul is the prince of this new realm, the controller of the transformation, laying down the rules to be followed by all his minions, and even dictating when they can be permitted to speak and what they may be permitted to speak about.

Making a story

Paul is putting on a performance here of a standard project manager identity, or 'archetype', which I refer to as the 'Enforcer'. His is a typical Enforcer story, founded in a narrative of creating order from chaos among a group of people who pursue diverse interests. His intent is to align them with his own aims. "We are in a mess", he effectively tells them, "and I am your hope of extracting us from this mess." To be the controller of the situation he needs to exhibit the status, power and behaviours expected of one who will control. He presents these credentials by laying down and enforcing the rules of engagement for the immediate scenes of the drama he is now stage-managing, the two meetings. So it is through his actions at the meetings that he announces his arrival on the stage of the project, and displays himself as that person who can say *"I took over the project"*. Through these actions he becomes the Enforcer for the project.

The identities revealed in this book all take a similarly active, interventionist form. They concern managers who have been through a challenging project situation, and chosen to tell their story about how they handled it. Their stories can all be understood within a single basic structure (already seen in Paul's example). They have a main protagonist, who experiences the events in his or her project life, and subsequently becomes the narrator of the story.

The following story elements are standard:

1. There is a 'situation' which our protagonist finds unsatisfactory, and is hence a challenge (in Paul's case, being sent to run a project having an uncomfortable degree of chaos).

2. In a project scene (or scenes) the protagonist claims a version of the 'truth' of the situation (in Paul's case the unseemly bun fights and chaos). Note there is no assumption that others share this understanding of what constitutes truth.

3. After scene-setting and early manoeuvres, he or she proposes a course of action and persuades the audience of the rightness of this course (in Paul's case through the introduction of regulations on behaviours at meetings).

4. In putting forward a proposed course of action, the protagonist establishes a managerial identity, the person they have become to be able to compel this action (in Paul's case, his version of The Enforcer).

In combination these final two elements are crucial to our journey of understanding. Our protagonist is presenting two forms of sense. Through his statements Paul establishes the situation as being a matter of chaos and bun fights, and he establishes himself as an Enforcer, the person who has the authority to assert this truth and act on it. Thus these two forms of sense, of the state of his project and of the person he is, are symbiotically linked. They sustain each other, and so must be understood together.

This mode of analysing pronouncements in terms of the speaker's social identity is especially useful in spheres where individuals are attempting to progress in a career. In a managerial environment there are frequent uncertainties and challenges, and decisions to be made. To become managers we must experiment in making managerial statements, speaking out to explain the sense we make of the current situation. Hence we are simultaneously experimenting with the possibilities for what our own managerial identity might be. Paul, in his story above, appears to be fairly practised in the arts of being an Enforcer, but in other examples we shall see individuals learning to be managers: trying on the hat of an identity, and negotiating their entitlement to wear it.

What it takes

We shall be discussing the world and life of Enforcers and other archetypes in more detail later (chapters 4 to 9). However in order to establish our principles it is worthwhile considering, in general terms, what Paul brings to his scene to establish his position successfully.

Firstly we should note some absences. There are matters such as ethnicity, gender, social class, etc, which might be thought central to personal identity. Could a woman perform the same manoeuvres? Are Paul's class and ethnicity relevant? Does Paul's physical appearance affect the plot? They are not mentioned, so it is probable that Paul does not consider them relevant to his position, or to his story.

And if these personal attributes are not relevant, what about Paul's identity as a trained project manager? Is he qualified? Is he a Chartered Professional Project Manager? Again these do not appear to be relevant, at least in Paul's eyes, and in any case, the standard toolkit artefacts and techniques, taught to project professionals in their training, do not figure in this story. It appears that his professional identity is not important.

What does appear to be significant is the business context, in the form of the programme of work and meetings, and the hierarchy of contractual relationships (which Paul takes care to explain with diagrams and charts attached to the text of his story). Paul's identity at the start of the story is founded on his standing in the organisation of the prime contractor, and particularly his relationship with his boss, the person who sent Paul into this situation when he found that he could not himself attend. That trust, from his employer, is the starting point for the story, empowering Paul to embark on his quest to be an Enforcer.

Also of great importance are Paul's personal strengths, his ability to deliver a simple summary of the situation, and his command of the narratives that go with an enforcement style of management. We should particularly note his rhetorical skill in constructing and imposing the central duality that underpins his argument, the choice he makes his audience take, between the *"dirty washing"* of chaos and the *"credibility"* of order. That rhetoric also serves to assert his identity, as the bringer of order.

In summary, there is an array of resources that Paul needs to have to hand, which he has chosen, developed and assembled specifically to enable him to play his central role in his story.

A person-centred perspective

I have gone into my interpretation of this story in some detail at this early stage to assert an important principle about my chosen perspective on identities, and to differentiate it, as clearly as I can, from the mainstream view of project managers put forward by the promoters of the profession. There will be those who ask why my style of story analysis is necessary. The institutions of the profession have already laid down, in some detail, their profile of the person holding that carefully defined position, the Project Manager. It covers the possession of the massive technical toolkit and the skills of leadership, negotiation, team-building, communications, etc befitting a 21st century manager.

The problem with this idealised identity is that such a person does not exist. Active managers (those who engage in the argument at those crucial moments when uncertainty is to be transformed into decisions for action) take personal bespoke paths to their managerial positions. Their use of textbook competences is, as in Paul's case above, highly selective and purposeful.

In this book, founded on stories told by real-life managers, I accept no given assertions concerning what a project manager ought to be. We will find out specific truths about who a person needs to be in order to act, and to tell the story. This approach enables us to take a highly person-centred view. Real individuals, taking action to respond to real challenges, will be the source of our understanding. (NB It is to clarify this distinction that I have chosen to refer to an actual practitioner in the lower case as a 'project manager' and to the institutionally defined position as a capitalised 'Project Manager'.)

Being person-centred in our investigations is particularly pertinent to the question of objectives. The mainstream position is simple: that the idealised Project Manager has a single duty, which is to work towards the successful completion of the project, whoever has defined it, and however it has been defined. The Project Manager has no personal aims, and has no allegiance other than to the abstract concept of the project and its completion.

In the real social world of projects things are markedly different. Projects do not emerge miraculously from 'out there'. They are the products of power politics, of negotiations between different groups and factions. Real managers of projects are part of this world, and see themselves as acting on behalf of a particular group and its aims. This is not bad practice on their part, but a necessary survival strategy in a complex social world. Their existence as managers, their reputations, and their careers depend on their being part of a group pursuing some wider endeavour. Furthermore their status within such a group depends on having a credible identity as a project manager, one which enables them, like Paul in our example, to take decisive action and control situations in the interests of their allies. For a project manager handling a difficult situation, therefore, success is not defined in terms of today's project deliverables, but in terms of their own achievement in putting on a coherent performance as a manager within their social group and organisation.

In Paul's case this difference in aims is not particularly contentious, in that he is willingly acting as the agent of his employer, the prime contractor, and for this particular situation the interest of his employer appears to be aligned with the completion of the individual contracts of the project. But this alignment will not always be so simple. We shall see project managers re-interpret the aims of a project to support their own personal ends, and those of the groups they support. This is not blatant fraud, such as the diversion of money and goods to their own accounts would be, but rather a concern to put their own career and reputation among their peers – their identities as project managers – ahead of those of the project sponsors. Of this project sin, should the situation confront us, we are all guilty.

This person-centred perspective is in a sense liberating for project managers. The behavioural prison walls erected by the profession, pursuing in its singular purpose through mechanised procedures, have been breached. We do not have to believe that the project is all, nor that we must follow that set of robotic rituals laid down by our high priests. We can find our own way, construct our own identity, be the person we choose to be, just so long as we can find ourselves a credible persona and mode of action, and can find the resources necessary to play our part on the project stage.

However while Paul has indeed thrown off the shackles of the profession, he remains, we must observe, tightly bound to the agenda of his employers and their commercial interests. At first sight his role as the Enforcer may appear to make him a person of power and influence, but he is at the same time an agent in a tightly bound relationship of dependency. The company that employs him needs him as an Enforcer to bring other parties into line with their interests, and he in turn, to acquire that essential credibility and attach it to his person, needs the company to grant him the right, the opportunity, and the authority to go forth and enforce.

So the environment for project managers is neither as suffocating as we might fear, nor as libertarian as we might wish. We will find that the performers' options are constrained, not so much by professionally defined norms, but rather by the agenda of the social groups on whose behalf they act. But within these limits we will see a wide spectrum of possibilities. Just as an actor on the stage can recreate and re-interpret a role, so our managers can find a freedom to develop and negotiate their own way of playing the project manager. The world of projects is an arena of possibilities for action, not a robotic or tightly constrained practice.

The central concern of this book is therefore the matter of how one speaks and acts to become, and establish oneself as, a manager in the world of projects. I will set out how this is done, in general terms, and through six archetypes. In this way I shall reveal to those who would wish to be project managers, or enhance their current playing of the role, how these archetypes can be performed on the project stage: the allegiances and alliances they must secure, the valuable resources they may acquire and bring into play, the rhetorical skills that can further their influence, the strategies that must be deployed, and the tactics that can make them effective.

Through personal stories about their struggles we will see real-life project managers constructing their managerial identities, and their careers. I hope this will give useful guidance to those who would follow them.

2. BEING A PROJECT MANAGER

Emerging as a manager

A managerial identity is created in action, by speaking and performing in workplace situations that are in some way challenging. But who takes these decisions to speak and act? How do they choose their opportunity to put a new persona on display, and what are their options for the direction they might take?

To tackle these questions we will start by re-looking at an extract from Paul's story in chapter 1, describing his moment of action:

> *After this meeting, I took over the project ... At the end of the meeting (at the start of any other business) I emphasised the fact that we needed to present a united front in order to be seen as credible suppliers (I used the metaphor of "not washing our dirty linen in public") and then laid down some ground rules for the next day.*

Paul's action here, driving his emergence as an Enforcer on the project scene, appears straightforward. He has been put in a position of responsibility and has found a place and a time to bring about his transformation, in front of his colleagues, into this new mould of manager. The 'place' he has found for his performance should not be understood as merely the physical location and the event that is this particular meeting. It also encompasses the state of the project, the opportunity the situation gives Paul to articulate his truths about the project, and hence establish his own position.

For others the situation is less tangible, and can take time to crystallise into an opportunity for new forms of action. In the next example Sally and her project team have been engaged by a client to implement a software development, and they have set to work on the agreed project:

> *As part of our research, we spoke with a number of the client's internal teams that would be impacted by the solution or that we would potentially have some dependency on. In the course of our research, we found out that there was a team that had been working on a solution that included a lot of overlapping functionality with the solution we were asked to build.*
>
> *As we learned more information, it became apparent that the internal team was continuing to build their own solution, even though they knew we were tasked with building something that duplicated a large portion of their work.*

At this juncture Sally could continue her work as a software project manager; she has a client, a contract, a viable scope, a budget, a skilled team. What more could a project manager want? Why do anything more? In fact she decides to move in a different direction:

> *I scheduled a meeting with the appropriate directors and managers to talk about the project we were asked to work on, and discuss next steps. During this meeting, I asked the question nobody else seemed to want to approach "Is one of these projects going to be killed in order to avoid duplicating effort and creating a repetitive user experience?"*

From a position of uncertainty Sally has created a tangible opportunity to find herself a new 'place' in the project world, which she tries out with her simple question which places the crucial decision in front of the senior managers. She has identified a new possibility for her life in the social and political business world, a new sense of who she is and the strategic player she can become.

On another IT project, Kieran has found himself in a difficult situation. He has been employed as manager of a large web development project. After some early uncertainties things go well, but then he discovers that people are not being paid, and soon he himself is only being paid irregularly. At this point many people would continue, heads down, with the work they are employed to do, while putting whatever pressure they could on their employer to get paid, and in all probability looking for a chance to leave and find a more reliable employer. Instead Kieran sees that he can embark on a new course, as an inquisitive strategist. He starts to investigate the murky business world of his employer, finding out what is going on, and carefully plotting his moves. He has found a new social space where he can develop his identity, and his move will be in the direction of becoming a different type of manager: a politically aware and savvy player on the organisational stage. A decision has been taken: one which will be career-changing.

My purpose here is not to describe in detail the new-found roles adopted by Sally or Kieran (which we will find out later), but to emphasise the fact that they took personal decisions that set them on a new course in their managerial career. These opportunities arose from the ambiguities and uncertainties of their projects, and were there to be taken. Within their respective project organisations there was indeed a place of opportunity – the new identity and how it is going to be performed – for both Sally and Kieran, although perhaps not what their employers had expected for them.

Sometimes the change is more forced, and the challenge more evident because the existing state of the project is not tolerable; it is endangering the continuing good reputation of its manager. For example, Thomas who works for a contractor in the oil industry, has a problem when the client appoints a new manager to oversee his work, a person who turns out not to understand the line being taken by the project.

Thomas spends months trying to get this new manager into order, with consequent delays to his project, but eventually has to give up on this strategy and prevail on the client's senior managers to get rid of the obstructive manager. He later concludes, with hindsight, that he could have done better:

> I would have probably moved to getting a little bit more ruthless about the timescale on which I developed a dialogue in which the guy got replaced ...

So the difficult circumstances compel Thomas to transform into his new ruthless self, in his new place in the contract world (but perhaps taking a little too long to emerge).

We see in all these cases that a situation of opportunity for a changed identity – the person I can become – has been discovered lurking in the shadows of the project. Our managers have acted, finding a way they can define and take control of the current difficulty, and use it to feed their growth, becoming the person who has what it takes to handle that difficulty.

This is how it is, how people develop to become this or that sort of project manager.

Adversity and resilience

Sometimes personal growth emerges through resilience, through finding a way to respond to adversity. There may be a direct threat, and you as a manager may find that you have little choice but to defend yourself. The place in the organisation you now occupy – your existing mode of working – becomes unfit for habitation and you must do something about it. This happened to Sally on an earlier IT project, her first as project manager. At first she believed things were going well. However:

> Apparently, though I felt I had been developing good relationships with the development team, I was not having the same success with some of the middle managers. I had started to feel some negative attitude creep into some of the communications and meetings, especially when a certain group of middle managers were involved ... I found out ... that there was one manager in particular who was undermining my position by spreading doubt about my capabilities and experience.

This setback is a serious threat to her identity as a highly competent manager. She must find a way to recover:

> My first reaction to learning about and realizing this was disbelief – I had never been treated this way. Disbelief quickly turned into anger, which then turned into sadness. I withdrew for a couple of days as I attempted to process the situation and determine how to move forward.
>
> Finally, from somewhere in the middle of the confusion, anger, and disappointment, I saw ... [I needed to] grab hold of the steering wheel, and steer towards a positive outcome.
>
> ... I focused my energy on his direct reports ... working directly with the team members to understand their tasks and their challenges, thus educating myself enough to be an informed advocate of the team. On a daily basis, I sat down with each member of the development team ... Team members started to feel comfortable coming to me to discuss issues, knowing that I would do my best to help resolve those issues ...
>
> My investment in the team dynamic and team relationships slowly but surely started to pay off. When asked for feedback or even when spontaneously in informal discussions where I would be mentioned, they had good things to say, and the results of our work together were reflecting in the team's delivery ... I had gained cheerleaders ... Eventually, the manager who started out doubting my ability to do the job started to treat me with more respect, and even gave positive feedback on my work to my manager.

In this long extract Sally expresses her dismay at the way she is being treated, and makes it clear that she can see no alternative but to act. It reveals important lessons about personal resilience, the ability to bounce back in response to a reversal of fortune.

Confidence is of prime importance, but often a workplace challenge takes us into a new zone, where our existing mode of working, where we are already comfortable, is clearly not good enough. Confidence therefore depends on finding a strategy for moving forward, and for that we need a thinking space, a place of withdrawal where we can pull together our reserves, reflect on our strengths, and prepare to renew our efforts. Sally, we should note *"withdrew for a couple of days"*, and in adversity we often need this retreat into ourselves. This act of withdrawal is not necessarily about physical separation. It is primarily a mental process. We must find a sense of detachment, away from the fray of our day-to-day problems, where we can, as Sally puts it: *"figure out how to remedy the situation"*.

The creation of a private personal space can be particularly important for project managers who are rowing against the tide of the profession. The world of projects is peopled by many who have an obsession with order, control, budgets and targets (for example our project Enforcer, or politicians who need to prove their managerial control). But some project manager performances, as we shall see, may demand a strikingly different approach: taking time, reflecting, opening up new ideas. Such a performance requires inner strength to resist the frequent challenges, and a personal space where confidence can be nurtured and recharged.

Resilience also needs social support. It is difficult to bounce into action if we feel we are alone in our struggle. However we often start out in precisely that state, with nobody aware of our plight. Our first need is to find allies, and particularly allies in the field of our battle. Rather than take on her main detractor directly, Sally focuses on individuals within the project, and brings them round to be her *"cheerleaders"*. Often the best strategy of resilience is to work on relationships, taking on power through its channels – the capillaries of the project work – rather than at its apparent source, the individual who may at first sight appear to be wielding that power.

Foremost for resilience, however, is having a sense of purpose, a certainty in our strategy, the direction we are taking and the motivation to see it through. This strength is often described in terms of the need to have a personal story. Motivation comes from a determination to be this person – a confidence in who we are – despite the obstacles that are in our way. In our search for personal growth however we need to look beyond who we are today, and develop a story about who we might become. We need to have a picture of the place we are going to occupy as we emerge from our difficulty, and the story of how we will become that person. This is what Sally has actually done in those *"couple of days"* when she withdrew. She has constructed a story of herself becoming engaged, immersed, people-orientated and much appreciated, the identity we then see her performing when she has successfully defended her position.

This progression, from the story about who we are now to the story of who we are to become, calls on our adaptability: our ability to change and become the person who can occupy that new managerial role. Tactically this approach is very important, not only because it carries better chances of success, but also because it re-shapes the agenda of our conflict. What started out as our attacker's story, expressed in terms of our weakness and deficiencies, becomes now a story of our own, describing our journey of recovery and our transformation into a stronger manager.

Adversity and our resilience to it are thus put to use as the drivers of our personal change and growth.

These principles of resilience are well recognised, but perhaps often misapplied. The self-help literature is rich with epic examples: people who survive aeroplane crashes in the wilderness and bring the passengers to safety, or soldiers who lose a limb but later overcome their loss to trek to the South Pole. We might be forgiven for thinking resilience is about major acts of heroism, responding to major disasters and life-threatening incidents. Resilience of this sort is for superheroes, and beyond the experience of normal mortals. In fact, as those who manage projects will be only too aware, the cycle of challenge and response is unremitting. Daily, things happen that threaten to throw us off course, and daily we make decisions on whether we can afford to let them pass, or whether we can resist and, in doing so, grow.

Decisions of speaking and acting

And at such occasions of opportunity to advance, not everyone decides in favour of action. In difficult situations, either of project uncertainty or of suffering a personal setback, many people, perhaps even a majority, do not take up the challenge. The personal growth option, taking these difficulties as opportunities for a new mode of working that will carry them forward, is often rejected. People may go on numerous training courses, gain all manner of qualifications, describe themselves as professional project managers, and yet still never make those moves that can take them to their managerial place. They will carry out the bureaucratic functions of project management, complete forms and schedules, and prepare reports about the decisions (and failings) of others, etc, but never themselves exercise any power of decision.

For some observers it is tempting to explain this anomaly in terms of human strengths and weaknesses. Perhaps there are two sorts of people: those who spring into action at times of uncertainty or adversity, and those who wait for others? However there are many good reasons why people may opt out of taking on a workplace challenge. It is tempting for those who have been successful at the career game to think that everyone is playing the same game, and that the rest are therefore just less able than they themselves are (a fallacy much to their liking). But life offers many other options. Employees thought by their employers to be lacking in initiative are often engaged in adventurous sports, or running social clubs, away from their workplace. They have discarded the career option, quite reasonably since it is often an unpleasant and stressful ordeal, rather than failed at it. They have found something better to do with their energy and their lives.

Others may have managerial aspirations, but fail to make progress. Much decision-making is competitive between different parties. Established managers often don't get their way, but they then move on to the next challenge. It is easy for new managers to lose heart and retreat into the shadows. There are personal risks that come from speaking good sense when it goes against prevailing thought.

In my next example, Louise, a psychologist, has joined a small project team delivering an organisation change programme to a corporate client. Their strategy is one of nurturing close relations with the client organisation's managers. However a new Human Resources (HR) Director is appointed and Louise's understanding of psychology makes her aware that the atmosphere is changing and a different strategy is needed:

... and it suddenly dawned on me ... that we had a sudden

> *change in HR culture and that this HR Director might just not want that very intimate relationship with us as suppliers but might actually dislike it ... and that what she wanted was quite a formal structured presentation. ... And I was trying to advise my colleagues on this and I don't think they really heard me ... So I talked to them about ... the evidence I'd gathered ... and was out-voted.*

Louise is over-ruled by her colleagues. She has spoken good sense, but the circumstances are not right for her good sense to be appreciated. But she is soon proved right when the new HR Director takes their team off the project. She might well take this setback to heart, and not bother to speak her brand of sense in future. However in her case the experience, of having been right but ignored, emboldens her into becoming more confident and she moves on resiliently to her next assignment, where she will assert more truths revealed by her expert knowledge, and this time be heard. To move forward on a career path we need this sort of determination.

So in summary, some press on. They take setbacks such as being ignored or being insulted, and build on these to strengthen their resolve, and grow their identities as managers. For others, the hassle of management existence is too much: they look elsewhere for personal growth and fulfilment.

Moments of fluidity

I have drawn attention in this chapter to a number of personal decision points. We have seen managers faced with the discovery that their current way of working cannot resolve a problem confronting them. We have seen managers who are being denigrated or undermined by their colleagues, and potential managers faced with difficult workplace situations where they want to find a voice, but may stay silent.

I regard each of these crisis points as a 'moment of fluidity'. At such a moment we have a choice, and that choice determines the course our career will take. There is a junction in our path ahead; we choose which route we will follow. We may well have little idea of where that path will ultimately lead us, but we have a choice to make.

I could apply this principle to any of the examples we have considered. If we take the case of Sally, we can ask what happened when she withdrew in response to being under attack at work. She returned after a few days in her new mode, the engaged, people-orientated manager. But in those days of withdrawal she had made a personal choice. On returning, she could have played a passive role, just accepting the insults and letting her career ambitions lapse. She could have looked for some allies and some manoeuvres to get back at her attacker. She could have read the small print of her contract, or hired a lawyer, and made a complaint. She could even have stayed in bed and waited for someone to come to look after her.

We can see that each choice is determined by the individual's understanding of their new self. For Sally, the alternatives *"... seemed to be 'cheap' ways of relieving myself of the responsibility of actually taking ownership and dealing with the situation at hand."* She had a clear vision of the person she could become.

Looking back later that choice will often appear inevitable. As people gain confidence in a new direction, the chosen path is full of promise; the alternatives they rejected will fade.

But observation of project life shows that the possibilities are usually quite varied. As developing managers, we need to believe in those alternatives, that our career has its moments of fluidity, moments that provide opportunities to take the initiative in determining our future courses.

Project manager archetypes

Having expressed our understanding of those who choose otherwise, it is now time to ally ourselves with the committed careerists: those who choose to persist, and seek meaning in their life through climbing the management tree. These are the people I aim to support. We will next look at the alternatives, for careerists, in terms of the places they can inhabit: the types of project manager they can plausibly be.

Of course there are infinite possibilities for identities. What we find, however, is that those possibilities have a limited number of distinct forms, which are the project manager archetypes. These can be thought of as modes of performing the role. Managers inhabit diverse fields of work and projects, and they have diverse aims, personalities, skills, and tactics, but nonetheless each competent performance is framed within a broad coherent form that is an archetype.

The archetypes are not an arbitrary classification of managerial behaviours. Their existence as distinct modes of performance is a consequence of the basics of what it means to be a manager. The essence of management is about power: persuading, coaxing or compelling others to act in a manner that you judge to be preferable. And the manager's purpose in this, to recapitulate the opening argument of chapter 1, is twofold, concerning not only the work to be done (for example the project in hand), but also the development of the manager's identity. Managers emerge by exerting their authority at times of uncertainty. In our example stories we can see, in every case, the narrators becoming who they are by persuading others to take a course of action that supports their own aims.

The possibilities we have for exerting this influence are limited by socially recognised forms of authority, which are the accepted and acceptable ways we have to exert our will on others. That power of influence resides both in our person, and in our position in the power structures in which we operate.

For the purposes of this book we will focus this very general theory of social action on that very limited and specific world, the management of projects, and look at the archetypes: six varieties of managerial performance that people stage in order exert project power and hold sway in project decisions.

In brief the six archetypes are:

> **The Analyst:** Guides action by finding resolutions to problems and issues. Immerses in detail, interrogation and logical analysis with the project team.

> **The Enforcer:** Acts on behalf of hierarchical authority to create order. Plays on fears of chaos and disaster. Deals in systems of authority, contracts, rules, and the law, extracting promises and enforcing them.

The Expert: Has technical knowledge in a professional discipline, and a process to be applied. Acts to bring others into line with the process.

The Impresario: Leads a personal value-creating adventure, persuading others to join in. Operates through personal deals, rule-bending, and dramatic events.

The Master of Ceremonies: Generates widely based, inclusive social value. Operates through openness, pauses and reflection, and resolution of conflict through discussion.

The Reshaper: Uses the project as the strategic arena for own career. Operates through political understanding, making and breaking alliances, reframing the project (and changing the rules) when necessary.

Thus each archetype has its associated performance mode (and tactics), its allegiances, its core narratives and explanations of what project management is about. From its performers it demands particular personal strengths and the sense of value they bring.

Each archetype also has its vulnerabilities, those hazards of being undermined, however well the role is performed. These vulnerabilities are quite varied. For example the insult to Sally's competence in her tale of resilience threatens her very existence as an Analyst manager; hence her emotional reaction and strong response. Other archetypes may ignore such insults (although the Reshaper might look at the tactical advantage that could be gained), but they however have their own particular susceptibilities.

The archetypes are not determined by personal psychology, as personality types. Nobody is condemned to be a particular archetype because of their nature or their childhood nurture. We all have many identities (perhaps less managerial in style) outside our working lives, and in the project field people may have the ability to perform in several different modes. However to perform any archetypical identity, the particular personal strengths demanded by it need to be developed, nurtured and practised. There are many who will only develop the capability, or perhaps the inclination, to perform one such mode (but yet often follow a successful management career).

The archetypes should not be equated to mere management skills. (They are not 'the six skills you need to become an effective manager'.) In a challenging situation the person who offers a resolution must appear 'in character' with a singular coherent identity that enables him or her to play that one part convincingly, and to be that one person who has the authority to take control of the situation.

It is reasonable to ask whether the six archetypes reflect the complete possibilities for project managers, a question I cannot answer except to note obvious omissions. There is the project administrator, generating schedules and reports but little more, who I consider to be non-managerial and have already excluded from my interest. There is the paranoid jungle fighter. I have no research material for jungle fighters in projects, but I know from personal experience that such people exist. They will be noted in discussing the Reshaper archetype, but I have not provided any further description of how the role is played (and such players probably need no guidance from me).

The recognition of archetypes and their associated performances underlies the change of focus we can now make, from pronouncements about a standard idealised view of what a project manager ought to be, to our person-centred support to real-life managers. The archetypes exemplify the possibilities of how one can plausibly be a project manager. Understanding them can have immediate impacts, providing guidance on how to put on a performance with which one can take charge of the situation of the moment. Archetypes can also inform the navigation of a longer path, the topic of 'who I can become', and the journey of personal development that is a career.

The archetypes can therefore function as role models for emerging managers. Some might also be idealised as a form of 'project hero', the person who can save the project. Their primary purpose however is not about saving projects, but is to provide guidance, for their personal benefit, for those who perform as project managers. Those wishing to be project heroes can make their choice of which archetype may support their aim, but should take care and be sure to understand its potential pitfalls.

Towards being credible and coherent

From a project management perspective the scope of this book may look quite narrow, dealing only with the manoeuvring round project decision points. It might well be objected that there is far more to project management than this limited topic. But my aim is not to analyse the entire subject of projects and their management. My interest is in the lives and careers of managers. For them these decision points, their moments of fluidity, are matters of life or death. At such a moment, a person with ambition may emerge as a credible and coherent manager, or else fail.

In the remaining chapters of this book we will look at how these credible and coherent managers perform. The chapters describing each archetype are obviously central to this ambition. Before we reach those chapters there are some general matters of performance to be examined: the diverse resources and strategies that managers bring on to the stage to take their hold on the project plot.

3. GETTING HOLD OF THE PLOT

Identity and performance

Having decided to emerge into the limelight and put on a performance as a manager, we will now need to consider how our management identity is actually created, which is through its two components, resources and performance.

The personal assets that you can bring into action can be thought of as your identity resources. Your manager identity is the combination of these resources themselves and the performance you put on using them. So for example a project management qualification, or membership of a professional institution, is not in itself your identity. It is a resource that you will find more or less useful in support of the project manager identity you perform.

The principle applies to many of the precursors you bring to your project activities: your formal company status and job title, or the toolkit of managerial techniques you have to hand. All may have their uses, but they do not themselves carry the day. Your ability to act and to have an impact on a situation, the project manager you are, emanates from how you deploy these resources as you set about your performance in the project field.

In this context, resources are sometimes referred to as 'identity capital'. They are the investments you and others have made in yourself. Your identity is what you subsequently do with that investment.

In later chapters we will see how resources are deployed to support the performance of specific modes of management, the archetypes. Some archetype performances demand highly specific resources; unless you bring the right resources you will have no chance of being able to play that particular part. In this chapter I outline resources that are of general relevance to being a project manager, and how they are brought into play in a managerial performance.

Allegiances and narratives

Every project manager acts with a basic allegiance. Around any project there are interested groups of people, competing for power and influence, and seeking gains – their own conceptions of what constitutes value – from the project. Your allegiance is the answer to the question: "On whose behalf am I acting?" Or simply: "Whose project manager am I?"

This is not to be confused with the concept of the 'Project Sponsor', the individual who, according to the norms of the project management profession, is the custodian of the project (although on many projects such individuals are surprisingly difficult to find). If we consider Paul's story in chapter 1, there is clearly a customer somewhere in the background: the organisation that has procured the project and to whom its output will eventually be delivered. They may well be the formal Project Sponsor. However Paul's primary allegiance is not to them; it is to the senior managers of his own employer, for whom he acts as defender of their reputation as competent prime contractors. They are his backers. He is their project Enforcer.

These allies, for whom the project manager is acting, will have their collective agenda and narratives. While our project managers can tell their personal stories about their own projects and the challenges they confront, these stories are told within an environment of shared stories. I refer to them as 'framing narratives', our communal stories of who we are, and where we are going. So Paul's own story is about how he personally dealt with chaos, at one critical moment, in one specific project that was his responsibility, but it appears to be part of a wider story: about poorly controlled and overspent projects, about his company's journey of learning to handle such problems to become a reliable and trusted contractor. Paul's short story is embedded in the longer story of that company journey.

To take another example, here is Simon's introduction to a story of a looming project crisis:

> *The particular incident I [am telling you about] was part of a major hardware and software upgrade that [...] were carrying out for [...]. All of [...] had been completed and we were in the process of rolling out the new software to the regional offices. This particular office [...] had a reputation as being 'difficult' in both the relationship with [our company] and with their own management in [...]. The plan was to carry out the hardware upgrade during the week and we had a team of engineers replacing PC's for over 300 users during the week.*

Simon is embedded in his roll-out team, and we can see here the elements of their framing narrative, with its portrayal of the past and vision of the future, and their shared assumptions: the competence of their team contrasted with the groups of difficult people who inhabit the far-flung regional territories where they must deliver their hardware and software upgrades.

The language I am using here, the description of the organisational world in terms of 'framing narratives', is merely a way of making explicit some very basic points that are implicitly recognised by experienced managers. They know who they represent, and what is expected of them by their backers, and this compels them to adopt particular modes of understanding of the situation and how they must perform. This sense of being part of something wider, not merely an automaton operator of a project management process, is an important resource. It is the foundation of their power and authority.

These framing narratives also express the basic values that inform our managers and their allies: the things that are important to them. To retain their allies, successful project performers must act out those values.

The tools of the trade

Tools of the trade are central to the profession that is project management. It is the possession of this toolkit, together the associated qualifications, that enables people to claim their status (with capital letters) as a 'Project Manager'. When Project Managers complain, as they often do, that they wish that their profession was more valued by society, it is the artefacts and processes of this toolkit that they wish to be more widely recognised, understood and appreciated. For many of them this toolkit is their most important occupational possession, defining their status, and underpinning their credibility in the project world.

However while the evidence of your toolkit may help you get a decent job, it does not itself have intrinsic value in day-to-day performances. The value of project management techniques comes about through their use by project managers. It is the people who are of value to projects; the tools are there to help them perform effectively.

Many project stories, of how this or that challenge was overcome, are told without any mention of the artefacts of the trade. Effective project managers are highly selective in their use of their toolkit, taking well-honed techniques out of their bag at critical moments, as the following two examples show.

Firstly Paul has a problem with contractors, who are experiencing some difficulties and wish to slip their delivery date. Paul, as an Enforcer, wants to resist this slippage and keep them on programme:

> *My technical team leader and I called a meeting with the Prime hardware supplier. We took a copy of the programme on acetate, some marker pens spent the day doing some "what if" scenarios. We looked at the implications of slipping dates and its subsequent impact on the overall programme. By the end of the day the ... technical manager was starting to ask the right questions regarding the impact of the event on the whole programme and it was recognised that the small slip ... would have a major impact on the end in-service date (which was unacceptable).*

For the purposes of handling the challenge of the moment, the extensive plans and documentation of this major project have been pared down to what is immediately relevant, "the programme on acetate, some marker pens".

In Sally's IT project, where she identifies overlap between her project scope and an existing implementation elsewhere in the organisation, a similar reduction is used at the crucial meeting:

> The evidence used during this meeting consisted mostly of:
>
> a) Taking the list of requirements for the new project, and showing the screens of the existing implementation, in order to show the overlap between the two.
>
> b) Providing the business with the development team's allocation and the cost/trade-off to shifting their focus to developing existing functionality

So summaries, lists of requirements and cost allocations, are used to put forward, and win, the argument for a change in direction.

This issue of project management tools and techniques is often discussed from extreme positions. On the one hand some highly successful managers claim that they hardly use the standard tools, and that too much educational emphasis is given to them. On the other hand the guardians of the profession and the sellers of web-based project tracking systems (Paul's acetate and marker pens look decidedly outdated!) present them as the key to successful project management, to be used in full or your project will fail.

A performing manager will take a pragmatic approach. What really matters is to have to hand the set of tools needed on the day to put on a credible performance. This may be minimal, or nothing. However the successful performer needs sound knowledge of what is possible, and how to assemble and present this evidence, and may need a mass of detail in the background from which to extract what is needed. The small section of programme data that Paul presents so effectively has been extracted from a detailed programme. Sally's presentation of requirements and budgets is only possible because of thorough work previously undertaken to analyse requirements and costs.

The most simple of performances therefore may be built on substantial background knowledge and project administrative toil. The power of artefacts should not be underestimated. Although I have decided to eliminate the project administrators from our discussion of managerial performance, we must still recognise that their output of project data and documents is often drawn upon by our high performing managers (who might otherwise have to do the drudgery themselves).

Personal wherewithal

Each project manager archetype demands particular individual strengths from the person who plays it. When choosing to adopt a mode of performing it is important to be aware of one's aptitudes and values, and the strengths one may need to develop, and perhaps also have the honesty to recognise when one does not have the power, or inclination to perform this way.

In discussing the archetypes we will find many who thrive in their environment, for example Analysts who relish the experience of delving into detail, or Experts who gain personal validation from their special knowledge.

However others struggle when the archetype they are performing goes against the grain. Harry is expected to operate as an Enforcer, but is clearly uncomfortable:

> *I'll let them come up with a deadline ... [and then] being a believer in empowering people and not micro-managing I'm not then going to walk up to them in a few days' time and say "have you done it yet?"*

> *... However there's been such a dire lack of following through and delivering work that more of a micro-managing approach is unfortunately going to be necessary. And it's not something I like doing, but I'm going to have to ...*

So there is a discrepancy, between the empowering management style with which he feels comfortable and the tight supervisory management style now expected of him, which he struggles to resolve.

This problem is evident when managers find they need to reconcile the style they must adopt with their personal values. Early in her managerial career Sally relates that she must work out:

> ... *how to assert authority while staying true to my values of collaboration, respect, team spirit, and everyone having a voice.*

To function as an Analyst she must establish authority; she is the person who is working out what must be done by others. But for her personal well-being she must also find a role for her collaborative self.

For those who feel a degree of discrepancy these are difficult decisions. The alternatives appear to be rationalisation or gritting your teeth and getting on with the job (with varying degrees of conviction). The third alternative, to under-perform the role, will lead to worse problems.

For any performance, another important resource is having knowledge of the best tactical moves. Strong performers, we shall see, have understood and practised the craft of their archetype, and can play the part with ease.

A strong performer also draws on an understanding of the specific vulnerabilities that are inherent in each role: those weak points, where any opponents of your efforts may find a way to undermine you, with consequent damage to your power, autonomy, and, perhaps most importantly, loss of face.

Finally concerning personal resources, we should note the importance of a more general social repertoire. Throughout our working day we are called on to put on minor performances, for example modesty, deference, indignation, anxiety, or being at ease. These behaviours can have a big impact on a situation, but, like the professional toolkit, must be used carefully and at the appropriate moment. For example, a display of indignation at the right moment can have a dramatic impact (and indeed, every manager needs to be able to play indignation) but used repeatedly such displays will lose their effect.

Speaking: telling the story

At the heart of your performance as a manager is the art of speaking. Your influence over others comes from your ability to speak as a manager, to explain the current situation in terms that coax others in the direction of your choice. It is through influencing others that you establish your position as an effective manager.

The ability to create a plausible and compelling story is fundamental to the influence you can exert. The examples I have used to demonstrate how project managers perform are all based on such stories, constructed by managers, to explain what they did at a time of challenge. These stories, told well after the events, and perhaps with a degree of hindsight, have been tidied, the loose ends tied up, anomalies resolved. They demonstrate something that those of us who have worked on projects know very well: that project managers are very good at telling stories about themselves.

But in practice if you, as a manager, are to carry people with you, the essentials of that story cannot wait for hindsight. The story must be put together and told convincingly at the time of the events. The basic story you must tell is simple. It will reflect the values of your allies, drawing on their favoured framing narratives. It will portray the present, using selective evidence to explain where we are, and create a plausible account of where we are going; a direction in which you personally have the knowledge and authority to take us forward.

Problem? What problem?

Your portrayal of the present will be in terms of a challenge or crisis. Up to this point I have treated this matter of a challenge as though it is real, that it concerns a disruption to normality that is clearly troublesome and must be addressed. But where and how has this situation arisen? In the real workplace problems do not just somehow appear, suddenly discovered and evident to all. Their existence and nature is always contentious and disputed. We will claim that the situation is troublesome, but to whom is it troublesome? Your initial task in creating the story of the challenge is to create this sense of trouble by describing the present as being a problem: a reality that compels others to take notice and demand action. The depiction of present reality as a 'problem' is basically an attention-seeking device, used to draw others into your interpretation of how things are. Problems are designed, not discovered. Even your labelling of the state of affairs will have consequences. The situation is to be presented as being troublesome, but is it a problem, or an issue, or a dilemma? Or perhaps it is a paradox, or a conflict, or an ambiguity, or a confusion?

Your management performance is thus not only about how you act to handle a challenging situation. It is firstly about how you define that situation, and how you do so in terms that can support your plan and identity. Your intended managerial identity must influence your conception of the situation, and hence the approach then required to address it. If you are to be an Enforcer, then you must highlight the chaos. If you are to be an Analyst, then the problem you describe will be a state of confusion that requires your personal investigation.

In essence then, a 'situation' is a primary resource; your presentation of it as needing attention is part of your performance of your manager identity.

Rhetoric: dualities

The presentation of the nature of the 'problem' we face is an example of the rhetorical skill that project managers must display to gain control of decisions. This rhetoric is not a matter of creating lies to get our way. Such a strategy would expose us to a high risk of being found out and discredited, which would be a serious setback because credibility is vital. But we must take the lead, and make sure that our own take on the nature of truth takes precedence.

An important rhetorical technique concerns dualities. The purpose of stating a duality is to create an illusion, which is that there is a single criterion for choosing our course of action. By deploying effective rhetoric, a complex and messy situation is transformed into a simple binary choice, and one of these options is plainly unattractive.

Paul's explanation of his project crisis (chapter 1) in terms of "dirty washing" and "credibility" was a classic example, creating an implication that the strategy for going forward was a simple choice between disorder and order. The alternatives he made available to the project team were either to follow his lead, or else be seen as a sympathiser of the only alternative, chaos.

I list here, for reference, the principal dualities favoured by project managers in their rhetoric. They are:

1. Social conflict: us vs them. "My plan supports our aims, not theirs."

2. Vision: clarity vs confusion. "I think clearly, but the others are confused."

3. Asserting: standing ground vs giving way. "We are right, so must not give way to those who are wrong."

4. Reputation: credible vs dubious. "Our reputation is good, but theirs is poor."

5. Direction: on track vs off track. "We keep everything in order, but others are dangerously uncontrolled."

6. Flexibility: freethinking vs hidebound. "We are creative, but the others are constrained by convention."

The style of use for these dualities is to present ourselves and our plans as being on the left-hand side of the duality, and those who might disagree as being on the right-hand side, and so to be discounted.

Appropriate use of the dualities will depend on the situation at hand, but more importantly on the archetype we are playing. Any duality will be emphasised or ignored as the case demands. Indeed it might be argued that dualities 5 and 6 are in fact contradictory, but in practice both can be effective (although perhaps not at the same time). For example Ryan makes an argument for political flexibility and not being bound by the norms of project management:

> *senior officers ... [were] wanting to maintain the illusion of control and rationality therefore failing to allow sufficient leeway for realpolitik as part of the project manager's toolkit*

But when Chris successfully negotiates his crisis, he describes his project in terms that carry an unequivocal directional rigidity:

> *[the] wheels were already set in motion and it was like a train running on the tracks towards its destination*

Chris's example also highlights a common feature of a well-delivered duality, which is the use of ellipsis. The antithesis, the discredited option, does not have to be thrust in people's faces and is often more effectively left silent. Chris does not need to spell out the consequence if we fail to keep our wheels on their tracks. We all know that it is a crash, and crashes are unacceptable, and so whatever Chris's plan may be, with its rigid track-controlled constraint on our activities, it is the only possible way forward. The purpose of a duality is to silence the alternatives, and if we can achieve that without even mentioning them, then so much the better.

The evolving plot: work, time and negotiation

We have now outlined the essence of constructing a management identity: the assembly of personal resources, and the putting on of a performance. But to attain a managerial goal there may be many obstacles to overcome.

We saw earlier that while some people may already be recognised decision-leaders, the performances of many others are transformational: occasions of personal growth for their performers. If we are to adopt a new mode of performing then, by definition, we are not wholly ready when our story begins. Our sense of self may not initially be adequate, and we may not have the means to take control, to define and then handle the challenge. We need time to work out the person we can possibly be, assemble our resources and feel our confidence grow until we can present ourselves in our new mode of working with sincerity (or at least with the assurance of a competent actor). This growth can often be experimental, trying out new ways of speaking and acting, with setbacks and restarts before we achieve our managerial performance.

In experimenting with new ideas about the truth of a situation – that the project is perhaps in chaos, or off track, or in confusion – we will usually find ourselves up against other players, ready to discredit our efforts. Usually they will be following other agenda, acting as the agents of other power groups, acting out other identities.

If you set out in a new direction, then ultimately your story will reach a moment of 'articulation', an episode where your best endeavour of a statement will be presented. This is your version of the story so far, your claim to the existence and nature of a 'problem', the evidence that makes the problem clear and tangible, and the apparently rational argument for your preferred course of action. The argument will also assert that you yourself are the person competent to lead the way ahead.

The argument of course will not be strictly 'rational'. It will be based on a subjective desire to promote the interests of you and your backers, and give precedence to their agenda. However if others are to follow your lead they must be able to accept your argument as rational. Blunt power on its own will not prevail. It must be supported by your rhetorical skills, to provide a coherent and plausible explanation to which others can sign on. Often this claim to rational reasoning will be post-hoc, assembled to justify and legitimise the course of action which has actually been decided on the basis of your allegiance and (probably undeclared) managerial ambitions.

We have already seen several articulation episodes, without actually labelling them as such. Here are two further examples, both related by highly reflective managers, who have explicitly understood the importance of articulation and made it part of their conscious management thinking. Firstly Thomas, persuading a key manager to accept his proposed changes to the project to get them *"back to the script"*:

> *I just had a discussion with the key manager around a structured articulation ... I used that form of words because people articulate, start to articulate something, and it might be something that needs to be drawn out and it's an argument that takes time to develop and articulate it. And they will be deflected from it and drawn into something else*

entirely by the questions of the other side. And it was an articulation, written so that we could get back to the script.

So articulation is difficult, with others trying to deflect us but we must persist.

Secondly James speaks of a difficult negotiation:

It required a very, very calm head, because it all got very emotional, and it required a combination of I think articulate expression along with good anticipatory calculation, because there were a lot of different options floating around that were quite complex, but most importantly it required, despite severe antipathy between the parties, it required that communication was maintained and that dialogue continued in a positive sense even during the most difficult events.

So the articulation of sense requires pre-calculation and clear thinking to create a logical statement that can be used to prevail over emotion. James's statement also highlights the fact that although we may be in intense conflict over whose truth will prevail, we cannot back away. Our argument must be articulated in full view and then withstand the onslaught from those who are emotionally averse to what we have said so clearly. (Attentive readers will have recognised James's argument as a variant of the clarity vs confusion duality.)

A performance is not simply put on. Founded on hard work it emerges slowly into the world, gets defined and refined, disputed and eventually assimilated, over time, until that moment when it crystallises into the articulation of project sense that carries the day. And with it emerges that new self, the authoritative manager.

"Speak that I may see thee" said Ben Jonson; and, having yourself spoken, your new managerial self is evident for all to see.

4. PLAYING THE ANALYST

The Analyst: working out what to do

The Analyst mode of being a project manager has its origin in the simplest concepts of projects and their control. While the high priests of the profession formulate complex technical management tools, others follow a simple logic. A project has an end point, when something clearly defined will be delivered. The work to achieve this end can be subdivided into discrete tasks. These can be listed and specified, and assigned to competent willing people who will complete them. In this ideal world, project management is easy and obvious. You work out what to do, and then do it.

The Analyst attempts to take this naïve, utopian vision of a perfect project world and apply it in the real world. This transfer however is far from easy, because the real world is full of complications, interactions and unknowns. If we are to bring such projects into line with our basic principles, and create a simple list of tasks to be done, we will need extremely clever people who can work out what to do, and repeat the exercise whenever new information emerges as the project proceeds. Our Analysts are these clever people.

The approach of the Analyst embodies the principle of the 'controlling mind'. Emily is the project manager for the validation of a new drug in the pharmaceutical industry. According to Emily, her boss has told her (in her annual assessment) that she:

> ... *proactively engaged with the various functions contributing to the process and asked insightful and clear questions in order to understand not only the stated need, but what 'driver' under-pinned this.*

So Emily, in her project manager role, is the single person who will understand all. She will find solutions, at every turn, that address the project's needs.

Another important principle, also evident in this example, concerns trust. The Analyst needs the trust of those who are actually doing the work, who must provide good information in response to her *"insightful and clear questions"*. She must be a friend of the workers, who must trust her to listen and interpret their intentions and needs, and trust her to tell them what's going on, and to keep in line those tasks that interact with their own. If they do not trust her they may start dealing in half truths and not be open about their problems, and then the whole edifice of the controlling mind will collapse.

The person, or persons, sponsoring the project puts their trust in the Analyst to create a sound plan. Through the Analyst's efforts and competence, issues emerge and are resolved; problems are identified and solved; snags are discovered, and cleared. When anyone calls for help, the Analyst appears at their side, listening, and dealing with their troubles. Through these efforts the project sponsor's agenda, the delivery of the project, is transformed into a plan that is precise and rational.

There is thus a chain of trust. The Analyst trusts the workers, the project owner trusts the Analyst. Without this trust the Analyst cannot perform the role. The trust, however, is conditional. An analysis that is deficient, if found out, will lead to a loss of trust, and probably then to the Analyst's rapid ejection from the project manager's seat.

The Analyst therefore deals in mutual respect. However because this respect is conditional, the Analyst deals, above all, in being right.

Endowed with excellence and respect, our Analyst, the

controlling mind, can investigate the project and define tasks, arrange for their completion, and so deliver the project.

The Analyst in action

The essential rhetoric of the performance rests on the identification of 'problems', which will demand action from our Analyst, the clever, interrogating and analysing interventionist.

A 'problem', to the Analyst, is a departure, or a threat of departure, from that logical chain of tasks and events that comprises the project. The ideal project is at risk, under threat from all sides: snags, pitfalls, deviations, overlaps, inefficiencies, lack of effort, lateness, and rework. Above these threats hovers the traditional evidence of failure in the factory, the scrap. The project's enemies – the competitors, the media, people who didn't get the project manager job – will make their accusation: money has been spent on producing output that had to be scrapped. Analysts are afraid that any of these events or allegations could leave them, their team and interested managers, with egg on their faces. They must be constantly vigilant to keep it in order.

Problems are identified and interrogated through close interaction with those doing the work. Emily, for her pharmaceutical project, reports that:

> *I personally contacted every team member on a regular basis to ensure that they were on track with their deliverables and helped them to resolve any issues which could delay their delivery.*

Meanwhile Sally, in a completely different field, managing an IT development, reports that:

> *On a daily basis, I sat down with each member of the development team to discuss the progress they made since the previous day, what they were working on today, and what challenges and concerns they had.*

So it is clear that the interrogation is primarily of people, and is very close and personal. The truth lies with the people.

The truth discovered about the state of the project must then be presented. In putting together the argument for a solution, the action that must be taken, there are three important rhetorical contrasts, or dualities, that Analysts use in support:

Firstly the contrast between the rational argument and the protective. The proposal put forward has arisen from a careful and considered investigation of all that is relevant. Those who disagree are protecting their territory, and their argument is purely self-interested.

Secondly, the proposal will herald a change of task content. The contrast between the Analyst's recognition of the need for change and the unthinking resistance of those who disagree, can be highlighted.

Thirdly, the proposal will be set out carefully and with precision. Analysts can contrast the clarity, which infuses their plans, with the confusion, which will characterise objections made by others who have put in less work to develop their argument.

Tools and techniques are simple, directed purely at coordinating. It is a matter of listing and defining tasks and their scope. Sharon, who manages community events in local government, states her commitment to the use of a well-known and comprehensive project Standard, but then uses only a very limited subset of that standard to run her project.

> *I am an advocate of [The Standard] but frequently see it misused and over-used ... [For my projects I] ... basically followed a check list and used email to communicate progress. This had worked well ...*

To get action from their analytical efforts, Analysts must firstly make sure that those doing the work have understood the truth that has been revealed, and are acting on it. This is part of the close immersed relationships such as we have already seen practised by Emily and Sally in their respective fields.

However it may also be that the proposed new path needs additional resources, or different skills to be brought in. Then managerial action, from those more powerful in the hierarchy, will be needed, and the analysis must be presented to the overlords of the organisation to persuade them to move into action.

We earlier saw Sally seeking action from senior managers to deal with the overlapping scope between her IT development project and the work of an internal development team elsewhere in the organisation. At the meeting to present her assessment of the position, she first contrasts her objectivity with the self-interested bias of the opposing argument, expressing:

> *... concern that the business owner who owned the internal project would feel like the project had been taken away from them*

She then presents her own clear and detailed analysis of the situation, before finishing with a further analytical observation:

> *... providing the business with the [other] development team's allocation and the costs and trade-off [from] shifting their focus ...*

Or, in plain words, suggesting they get off Sally's patch.

Emily finds that resources have been diverted from her pharmaceuticals project, and presents her analysis of the consequences to those who are setting priorities:

> *... a lot of decisions had to be made in pressure situations. The best examples of these were when we had to decide to slash final review timelines and, as a team, conduct the final review in a 'locked-in' situation, as this was the only way the delivery could be made in time.*

This bit of jargon, the 'locked-in' situation, is quite intimidating, although I don't believe they were physically locked in. Whatever the degree of applied restraint, the strong choice of words shows how seriously the situation is taken. That can only happen because Emily has thrust a potent reality, a truth gem, into the faces of her managers.

These detailed and careful presentations to managers are attention-grabbing ploys. Each is an act of aggression to place a perhaps unwanted truth in the personal space of those senior managers. This ploy is an essential strategy of the effective Analyst, to generate the action that completes their analytical cycle. Competent performance of this move is central to success in the role. Badly played, the aggression will be resisted, the Analyst will be labelled as a trouble-maker, and managers will be reluctant to listen to the story they are being told, and probably refuse to act in response to it. Sally and Emily have each played their scenes skilfully, and got their desired responses, and so have been credited as a potent analytical forces.

And so, presenting his or her analysis, the Analyst drives the cycle from problem to solution to action. But then, every day that progress is made, new truths about the state of the project – its technology, its impacts, its complications, its uncertainties – will emerge. Analysts must repeatedly re-engage to check their analysis of the situation, and if necessary re-analyse and re-plot the path to the end of the project. Once complete, the analysis cycle starts again.

The Analyst's mode of operating is exemplified in the stories they tell, of projects rescued through their brilliant efforts. Typically these relate how inefficient plans were rationalised or consolidated, how disputes were resolved, how diseased tasks were cured (or amputated), how money was saved. Project processes and systems are downplayed in these stories. It is individual excellence, that of the controlling mind, that brings success. At the story's conclusion, the Analyst's sponsor looks good, and their faithful servant is showered with praise.

Inner life: being right!

The essence of the role is about being right, and letting everyone know we are right. Sally introduces herself with a powerful statement:

> *A few years ago, I was making the transition from junior project manager to taking a more senior role within an organization. I approached the transition with enthusiasm, excitement, and a passion for achieving excellence, ... excellence ... [being] doing the best that I could do with anything I was tasked with. As a project manager, my goal was to deliver a successful project that fulfilled its requirements, on time and on budget, while troubleshooting, communicating, and resolving any issues that stood in that goal's way.*

This 'excellence' might be thought of, first and foremost, as a personal trait, something ingrained in her personal identity, the sort of person Sally would be whatever her chosen profession or way of life. I suspect that in her case that may be so. But it is also a mindset that must be adopted by anyone who might choose to play the Analyst mode of managing a project. Those with a relaxed attitude to perfection outside the workplace will have to get into the perfectionist frame of mind if they want to wear an Analyst's hat.

The perpetual hazard is of losing the day. Sometimes we may find ourselves cast as being wrong, and then things will get difficult.

The first consequence of being wrong will be a disappointed protector. Someone has sponsored us in our managerial position, and has put trust in us. We have an obligation to be good, and to keep our moral authority as the person who will work it all out, the person who will point everyone in the right direction. Point in the wrong direction, and we have seriously let them down.

Worse is the possibility of being disregarded. Our strategy has been about getting attention, pointing at a 'problem' in some shape or form, and then putting our efforts into presenting its solution. What if the solution doesn't suit our protectors? Perhaps they have another agenda, and solving this project problem isn't top of their list of concerns. Perhaps they have their own biased objection because of some political agenda nobody has mentioned to us. Our gems of wisdom are not wanted. The Analyst can be like an enthusiastic pet cat, bringing presents to its mistress. Your present tomorrow may, to her, look decidedly like a dead mouse dropped on her clean carpet. The purpose of our being so clever was to get admiration; it is dreadful if we get rejected. We have already witnessed Sally's rejection, with influential people disparaging her competence and the trouble it caused her.

> ... there was one manager in particular who was undermining my position by spreading doubt about my capabilities and experience ... in communications (emails, etc.) ... he would take a condescending tone and approach.

Rejection hurts!

We may also lose the trust of the doers, those people we have got so close to because they are the source of our analytical knowledge. Our strategy depends on getting them to explain to us what they are doing, and we must understand it. Their knowledge and enterprise gets absorbed into our plans. They may react adversely, thinking they are being over-managed, and give us half-baked advice, or simplify issues that need more investigation simply to get us off their backs.

It is always possible that trouble is brewing out of our sight. When Sally found herself discredited she had to divert her efforts from the constructive pursuit of the project, and focus on a new diversion, an analysis into the plot to disrupt her. She was too slow to spot things going against her (but learned the lesson that in future she will need to keep a closer eye on everything).

Arriving at this state of neurosis we may also find ourselves asking questions about the basic competence of those doing the actual work. Perhaps they aren't as trustworthy as they seem. Perhaps they have missed a trick and have suggested something untenable, which we have now incorporated into our plan. We need to keep them under scrutiny; but perhaps not too close, because if we interrogate them too intensely, they will react badly, and we could lose our most important allies.

In the political world of projects we are also perpetually at risk from the alternative competing analysis. Someone somewhere, equally adept at the skills of analysis and its rhetoric, may have reason to go in a different direction, and present a plan, perhaps even to our own manager. We are always under threat of being discredited, under threat from people infringing work we thought was within the compass of our controlling mind.

For example Nick had his plant engineering project carefully planned, but went on holiday at a crucial stage. Caroline was put in charge while he was away, and took the opportunity to flex her recently developed muscles as a political operator. Nick found his position being undermined:

> *She had gone to the client's engineer and ... then returned to the office and made out that I had missed a crucial requirement. As a consequence they had fundamentally changed the design and we were three weeks behind*

programme.

I couldn't let her get away with it. Over the next three days I pulled together a dossier – the original brief, the correspondence, everything. I took short statements from all the engineers on the job. I sent my dossier to the senior managers and demanded their support. How could I continue in my job if I didn't have their complete trust?

Being an Analyst is hard work, but we see here that the work is an order of magnitude harder when we are destabilised. Nick cannot go back to his constructive project work until he has subdued the attack. He cannot tolerate the implication that he was wrong. He must go back to his Analyst's art and redouble his application of it: an analysis, a dossier, a presentation to his sponsors.

Sharon in her local government office was unsettled by a different sort of challenge; that of a new democratic culture. Her simple analysis and control methodology was threatened when her boss demanded a new openness, bringing community volunteers, untried, unreliable, into her world. Such people are not compatible with the Analyst's need for close working relationships and trust. Her response was desperate, deliberately running one of the volunteers on a very loose control to let him go wrong, almost disastrously. She ditched the success of her project (the volunteer can be blamed) but successfully established the principle that it is undesirable to open projects to such people, and restored her preferred tight management, through analysis and control, for future projects.

We heard earlier of the Analysts' favourite stories of project rescue. These examples of disruption show that we can add another story, that of the 'Slur on my Reputation'. The Analyst comes under severe and unwarranted criticism, under attack as being inadequate for the role, but responds with a very public demonstration of their excellence, and pursues all parties, opponents and senior managers, until they agree that the slur was unfounded. The Analyst's reputation is restored, unblemished.

For us Analysts it is difficult enough to be good and right all the time. But that pressure is compounded by the need to be vigilant in the political project world, anticipating and deflecting threats. Our project rescue story can suddenly be displaced, pushed aside as the story of our slurred reputation takes centre stage.

Another matter of concern for many Analysts is the nature of our relationship with our managers, which is one of high dependency. We are bound, as servants, to the agenda and strategies of our managerial masters. We are there to support them. Do otherwise and we will be replaced with someone more compliant. They, in turn, are dependent on us for the arguments they need to pursue their plans. Our brainpower delivers the justifications for their actions.

Some people are very happy with this type of working relationship. They look after their boss, who in turn looks after them, lavishing praise at the end of each rescue story. Many Analysts, perhaps playing for admiration, wallow in this praise, the reward for their excellence. Sally boasts of her many 'cheerleaders'. The more suspicious of us are rarely so comfortable, realising that any change in the wind can lead to a change in our well-being. We do not feel comfortable with being so indebted to those in authority, and like to have more independence of action.

My prime objective is to support those pursuing careers in project management. It is my view that the careers of those who remain as Analysts are rather limited.

Or Perhaps Moving On?

A project rescued through analysis makes a good story, a simple narrative about our starring role. The Analyst is clearly pursuing a socially valuable occupation. Some senior managers may be concerned, occasionally, by the amount of time Analysts spend preening their precious reputations, but they will nonetheless still respect and value them.

But behind the stories of project rescues there are personal stories. At good times these will be rewarding, about mounting pride in our abilities. But as Analysts our lives may often be dominated by energy-sapping struggles, as we pursue the aim of being perpetually right (and being seen as right). We must always be on our guard against trip wires and snipers, and we must work very hard to right wrongs. We can experience repeating cycles of depression and resilience, and these will ultimately take their toll. Some people may indeed retreat, taking their analytical self away from the public gaze, perhaps into a life of being right in private, but no longer a leader of decisions.

For those who persist in playing the Analyst, this role can become one of assertive, almost pugnacious, intervention, taking up project problems, picking up whispers of dissension or infringement, bringing them to the foreground, and then devising a solution: problem-and-solution episodes that may happen daily and take up most working hours.

However each and every one of these episodes involves a personal decision. If you are a resolute Analyst, that decision will always be to make the problem into an opportunity, which you will grasp, to play the scene in character, to launch into your Analyst's performance, hurrying as though there is no time to be lost to re-assert your identity. But it is a delusion to think you have no other option. Most important for self-reflection are those instances of serious crisis, when your role and identity are most under threat. That big crisis can provide an opportunity for change, the moment of fluidity, when you could do otherwise, and find a different form of action.

Most Analysts move on after a while, taking advantage of an opportunity to experiment. An analytical mind is a precious asset, but analysis, presenting that gem of truth to your team and to your management admirers, is not the only strategy. As an alternative you may find ways to calm your brain and press that obligation to analyse, the responsibility to work out the way forward, onto others. You can have impact, perhaps in ways that are more personally advantageous, without forever delving into details.

Even when they have moved on, Analysts appear to retain some nostalgia for the utopian appeal of the Analyst's world, that Garden of Eden of project management. We have already heard from Sharon, who actually undermines the moves of her organisation to develop a more participative approach in her attempt to get back to that ideal era, when she was the controlling mind and all was well. Harry, who we will soon witness struggling to play the Enforcer, expresses his unhappiness by harking back to that wonderful time when *"we could get a few of us together and work out what to do"*. The Analyst's world holds a nostalgic attraction for those who have left it, but today find themselves in a messy world they find less comfortable.

Ultimately those emotional highs of immense satisfaction and pride are short-lived. The Analyst's life is unrewarding for those of us who would rather be strategic actors and pursue a higher managerial status. For those with grand ambitions it is not really a career; it is better to move on.

It is also time for this discussion to move on, for us to leave our Garden of Eden and consider some more sinful performances, starting with the management charade that is the Enforcer.

5. PLAYING THE ENFORCER

The Enforcer: getting a grip

The Enforcer mode of being a project manager has its origins in the world of commitments, obligations and duties. Parties wishing to contribute to a project make promises, contracts are agreed, and the work is assigned. Project management is about arranging such agreements (formal or informal) and seeing that commitments made are honoured, so that the various parts of the work, and hence the project as a whole, are seen through to delivery.

Government development projects provide obvious examples of this world. Paul (whose story introduced the concept of management as performance in chapter 1) works within complex structures of prime contractors and sub-contractors. He is obliged to keep them in order and hold them to account for the commitments they have made.

On a smaller scale, Matthew has been engaged as project manager for a government-sponsored IT development project and trial:

> When I got into it I was quite taken aback by the state of things. A number of local agencies around the country had come on board to take part in the trial, and two software

> suppliers had been identified, but otherwise it was chaos. There was no business case, no single clear vision of what we were doing, and no specification of the software requirements. As a result the pilot agencies were going their own ways, inventing their own ideas of how it would work. There was no way this uncoordinated activity could lead to a meaningful trial that could be completed by the date that had been promised to the minister.

For Matthew (and indeed for anyone else willing to play along in this sort of politically dominated business) the position is crystal clear. A promise has been made to a figure of authority, and he is accountable for it. In order to deliver his promise he must extract equally clear promises from the parties to this IT development and trial. They must immediately be made to define exactly what it is they will do, and then he, Matthew, must ensure they deliver exactly what they have committed to, and hold them to their promises. Given these obvious truths, his first action following his appointment is entirely predictable:

> I hammered out a project scope with the agencies and suppliers – something properly defined that we could reasonably hope to achieve in the time allowed.

For this type of project management activity, the hammer alluded to by Matthew is the implement of choice. How else can people be brought to order? There is a chain of authority, and a chain of commitments must be made. If one link in that chain fails, the whole edifice will collapse, and chaos will return.

The language and thinking of this project territory is obvious to anyone picking up a newspaper or listening to a news broadcast. A politician issues a statement claiming that the previous administration has let a government project go adrift, with "costs spiralling out of control". However the new broom has now arrived and will sweep away this indiscipline and bring everything under control. The guilty have been blamed and removed from the scene. A new managerial power has been established. All the politician now needs is a force that will produce the required disciplined state of affairs, in which all is brought into order. And the name of that force is Project Management.

The weaknesses in this argument are apparent. The politician has not just invented project management, and there is no reason why the discipline should now be able control what it failed to control before. However this tool he now possesses, Project Management, provides the justification the politician needs to take action, to move forward, to make commitments to deliver something of social good, and to set up that essential chain of commitments from others.

Our archetype, The Enforcer, is the purveyor of this forceful discipline. He or she is the project manager who supports a person in the commitment chain (or at its head), someone with an obligation. The Enforcer is the agent of a sponsor. *"I was asked"* says Paul to introduce his story, and this sense of having been hired by someone, to perform an act of tough management on their behalf, pervades the identity of the Enforcer. At the core of the role is the possession of a credibility, to threaten (that hammer!) and enforce.

The political rhetoric, we have noted, presents this project world as inherently ordered, which is why it can deliver the goods, to time, and within budget. Without that rhetoric, the project will not get funded, and will not start. However the flaws in this enforcement model, with its logic of commitments and their fulfilment, can make our Enforcers vulnerable. Beneath that surface of order lies an undercurrent, the possibility of disorder. Projects are perpetually threatened by the imminent possibility of disruption. People default on their promises; plans turn out to be unworkable; and we will be dragged under into chaos.

I do not intend to imply that this style of organising work is intrinsically invalid. In many instances it is, in principle, eminently sensible. If I need a new bathroom for my home I will get an offer or offers from competent people, do a deal with them, and then expect them to complete the work at the agreed price, and I will do my best to enforce the agreement we made. That however does not amount to a performance as an Enforcer. Our concept of the performance of managers and their identities centres on the matter of a challenging situation and the person they must be to handle it. In the simple arrangements for my bathroom there is no significant challenge, and no real managerial performance is warranted. I am merely finding an organiser for the bathroom work. The essence of the Enforcer role is much stronger stuff; it is a performance as the bringer of order and control in situations where the application of enforcement is decidedly challenging.

The business world, especially that part of it connected with government spending, is rife with such situations. The drive for public accountability, and the desire of political leaders to demonstrate that they have a grip on things, leads to the setting up of projects where there is no possibility of a simple promise-and-delivery mode of running them. Our politicians demand order and control whether or not they have coherent plans that might make such control feasible. They advance their self-promotion by giving life to projects that are improperly conceived and prematurely born. When Paul finds he needs to exercise strong measures to bring his subcontractors into order, it is not because they are fundamentally hostile or untrustworthy, but because they are struggling to do the work for which they are responsible. Matthew, in his story above, has difficulty creating a definition of the project deliverables because the possibilities, the forms that definition might take, are hazy and uncertain. It is hard work to bring order in these circumstances, but the Enforcer pushes ahead to establish that order despite the obstacles.

The essence of being an Enforcer is the attempt to impose this management style across the board. It may be extremely difficult to get the commitments we need, or they may turn out to be worth less than the full currency. But our performance as an Enforcer is directed towards bringing those zones of freedom and uncertainty back into project restraint, those zones of inertia and dubious assurances back into order, all on track to complete the project.

Or if that does not work, we will ensure the blame for non-completion has been firmly placed elsewhere.

How to perform the Enforcer

I have gone to some length to describe the world Enforcers inhabit (or believe themselves to inhabit) because the perceived structure of that world determines how they must perform. But what does the Enforcer, our trusted agent who has been allocated to the job, actually do, especially when those flaws in the logic of their project model manifest themselves?

The first matter of importance is about having authority, about being asked. The first question we must answer is simple: whose Enforcer are you? Usually this is obvious. Paul has been asked to sort out the chaos by his boss; Matthew has been asked to deal with the mire of uncertainty by a government minister. These firm foundations for their positions, the tangibility of their sponsors, make the necessities of their performances clear (although not easy). If this clarity is lacking, the Enforcer often struggles.

The Enforcer speaks the rhetoric of disruption. Everywhere there is impending chaos, or default, or inaction. To be Enforcers we must talk tough. We are perpetually "getting a grip on the project". Harry, who we shall see soon struggling with project inertia, decides the time has come to *"grab the project plan by the scruff of the neck"*.

Our basic rhetorical resource, our primary duality, is thus about the contrast of order and chaos. At any point of decision the only option we will propose is the order we can bring. The only alternative, to be avoided at all costs, is chaos, usually represented by various unreliable defaulters, or those who unreasonably resist our regime of order.

Paul reports a problem with a supplier:

> *The Hardware supplier wanted to slip a delivery date by a couple of weeks. This ... would have a major negative impact on the whole programme.*

So the supplier's view is immediately discredited.

People who just don't want to be organised are another example of that potential chaos. To an outside observer such people might look like good committed enthusiastic workers, but if we wear the Enforcer's hat they represent a severe problem. Matthew was moving to rein in such individuals as he *"hammered out a project scope"*.

Keith is Project Manager for a project to develop an innovative industrial machine. His efforts to impose strong project order are challenged by an engineering manager who:

> *... was forever submerging the team in endless debate, and*

creating needless turmoil

Keith's feared 'turmoil', of course, is another variety of that chaos which we fear is always about to envelop us. To neutralise these people, those who are always wanting to discuss other possibilities, never wanting to be pinned down on getting something done, they must be devalued as people, presented negatively as those who are *"forever submerging the team"*. To move forwards towards our ideal, the ordered project, we must discredit their thinking as *"endless debate"*.

It can be difficult to establish a reputation as an effective Enforcer. Experienced players of the role can bring evidence from past projects into their argument. They have seen projects fall apart because their advice has been ignored; they have seen projects rescued through their interventions. Beginners, such as Matthew, may struggle to claim this aura, but can manage if they act with confidence, and supplement their own limited experience with heroic stories borrowed from others.

The key component of the performance is persistence. It is not enough to act to bring order only when confronted by major incidents. Your enforcing identity will not be established and you will lack that essential credibility. The 'me', the person who demands and expects order, must be visible and known as such to others working on the project before that crisis decision is needed. All project scenes must be treated as opportunities for you to act out your persona. Thus Paul's action at his first project meeting (witnessed in chapter 1) was to establish his position by laying down some rules for meetings.

Harry is manager of a project, in local government, to deliver new information systems to support social services. He is plagued by a debilitating form of 'chaos':

people offering advice and being critical of one another, but no actual work delivery

Harry decides to re-invent himself as an Enforcer. His first action is to display his new identity, as Paul did, at a meeting, telling all what may or may not be discussed at the meeting:

That's the new me, asserting a standard agenda for the project board ...

So while these behaviours are, on the surface, about meetings and how they are run, they are simultaneously about using these meetings – scenes where the players in a project come together – as opportunities to present and establish an Enforcer's identity: to lay down some rules, and by doing so show others the sort of person you are. Conversely a failure on your part to present an Enforcer's identity on even trivial occasions could compromise your ability to claim the role when significant project incidents need to be handled. The pursuit of tight organisation – making rules, creating systemised processes, etc – must go on at all times.

The Enforcer's toolkit contains the artefacts of order, the documents that detail and fix those imperatives: deadlines, specifications that close down options, contracts with penalties for defaults, and records of promises and of failures to fulfil those promises. On larger projects a core project team will provide the Enforcer with important support creating these project artefacts. You will need documents that closely define the work to be done, and evidence to underpin arguments about the dire consequences of relaxing discipline. It can be argued that the standard toolkit of the project management profession has been designed with Enforcers in mind; they are its greatest enthusiasts.

All efforts relating to project order are matters of urgency. If things should go wrong later and the project gets behind schedule, then any time spent pondering about what to do will be seen as contributing to that delay. Any time the project spends in a state of uncertainty may be claimed against you, and attract the inevitable blame that will arise to yourself and your backers. Allegations of confusion – "they didn't get the job in order" – can seriously undermine your future credibility.

Matthew, as we saw earlier, moved instantly into action and *"hammered out a project scope"* as soon as he was appointed. He needed to be seen to be in control, and his fast action was necessary to show everyone that he was there, and the sort of project manager he was going to be. Much later he became aware of other consequences. In the calm of retrospection he noted:

> *I've shown what project management can achieve in a*

difficult situation, and shown that I can do it. ... [However] I've given the impression [my predecessor] left everything in a mess and I sorted it out ... In fact he was an incredibly creative man.

So by acting quickly he had established a formidable credibility for himself, but he realises the performance of that self has had other, perhaps less desirable, consequences. However in relating his story Matthew, while absolutely direct in stating the fact of his own success, alludes only tentatively to the possible negative consequences of his behaviour. The rhetoric of success pervades.

Whatever the project outcome, Enforcers will claim credit for some form of positive outcome achieved through their intervention. Such claims are the cloth from which the credible Enforcer is tailored.

The creation of heroic stories is an important part of the Enforcer's performance. In any gathering of project managers (and elsewhere) they can be heard trumpeting their achievements. Favoured stories are variants of the Getting-a-Grip Story:

> The defaulter sorted story
> A contractor claims that the job cannot be delivered, to specification or to programme. The Enforcer persuades them that they have no alternative and compels them to take whatever additional action is necessary, at their own expense. Within 24 hours they are back in line.

> The chaos rectified story
> It is discovered that various parties to the project are 'doing their own thing' and going in different directions. The Enforcer bangs heads together and, within 24 hours, gets them to promise new, and consistent, work scopes.

> The drifters and boffins story
> The project is plagued by people who are too clever and cannot keep focused. The Enforcer makes them commit to firm and clear deliverables. This is a war of attrition, which the Enforcer eventually wins.

Note that any of these stories might be less than satisfactory from the point of view of the project and its contribution to the wider social world. However they all serve to create or reinforce the identity of the Enforcer.

Inner life: being in control!

Life as an Enforcer provides much that is rewarding. Envisaging yourself as the hero of the project can be an attractive proposition, and gives a sense of achievement. Paul, having got the meetings into good order, goes on to claim that:

> *from then on the two meetings ... became more focused, structured and positive ... and we delivered the programme to time*

He obviously feels good about himself, and we can share his pride.

The life of the Enforcer is about overcoming unreliable workers and contractors, bringing general chaos into good order, and taking on and reforming people who lack our own sense of direction and purpose. If we are Enforcers, we see the world as being full of people who are just not good enough to live up to our standards. There are too many creative designers who just don't understand the need to focus on delivering, and disorganised people everywhere who don't recognise the importance of keeping their promises.

Every time we encounter such weak thinking, it is an opportunity to go into action and bring the miscreants into line. Subsequently we will get the chance to tell the story of yet another successful foray into the land of the unreliable, the unfocused, the foot-draggers, and all manner of lesser mortals.

That is what we like to think. The basic problem is that it might not come off. There are other powerful forces at work in organisations. The completion of the project is not all, and we might not easily get our way.

On Keith's industrial machine development project we have seen very briefly how he needed to deal with an engineering manager, who obstructed Keith's efforts to bring the project into line by perpetuating that *"endless debate"*.

Keith is in fact in a very difficult situation. He has been sent by Head Office to a remote factory to bring some order to the excessively protracted, but innovative, projects that are carried out there. Keith's authority to bring control is invested in his professional Project Management qualification, and the ordered management process he can apply. This process, he tells the local managers, they urgently need. However his Head Office masters hold little sway in this province of the company. The local managers are expert in their highly specialised field, and regardless of Keith's appearance on the scene, with his process, they continue to work in the manner they prefer. Keith prepares specifications and detailed plans, publishes them, and issues threats about what will happen if the plans are not followed. But the local managers can ignore him, sending work off at tangents to Keith's plan, and they will, if they see fit, return to the start and revise the project scope if they discover a more innovative option. That is how they work.

Keith can claim all manner of benefits from his project management process, but he is impotent because he lacks the basic power of an Enforcer. He has been asked to enforce, but by someone who is not present in the local power structure. He is vulnerable because he has no sponsor or protector on the battlefield of the day. But nevertheless he persists in fighting on, and eventually the local engineering manager decides that the flexible phase of development is over, and considerately backs away to let Keith apply his project management discipline to the final stages of the project, the production of a prototype machine.

On his social services project, Harry's problem with chronic inaction across the various departments has a different cause. His managers have him told him to be assertive to make sure all managers are brought into order. His efforts to make meetings more organised were his demonstration of that new assertiveness he is to display as Project Manager. He gains some ground on producing the system specifications:

> ... *we've all acknowledged that the 15th March is the absolute, absolute deadline. And everybody is committed to that, so I think I've managed to win on maintaining the pressure* ...

However soon afterwards, at a meeting with the software suppliers, his plans to meet this deadline fall apart:

> ... we put it to the suppliers in that session that the 15th September is our required go-live date ... Based on your experience, suppliers, is that a sensible timeframe? And ... there was talk of "hmm – systems never go live in September because of school holidays" and ... they all agreed that actually Christmas is a more sensible go-live target.
>
> ... The reaction of the project sponsor was "Ah, thank goodness for that. That gives us a bit more time ... We were intending to put the ITT out at the end of this month, but I think there's a lot more work we need to do on it, so we can push back on that."
>
> But I had the wind knocked out of me when I saw all the project team sinking back in their chairs and suddenly feeling all good, about oh we've got loads of time now.

What is going on? His managers have demanded that Harry imposes discipline, but as soon as his colleagues see an opportunity for indiscipline they have grasped it. It is understandable that Harry is deflated; his purpose has been destroyed, his identity undermined. For whatever reason the managers are not particularly committed to the project Harry has been asked to enforce. But his colleagues are happy for him to continue the pretence of tough project management, and presumably for him to take the blame if the politicians later come under pressure for their non-delivery of this new information system. When the chickens eventually come home to roost it will be the project manager's failure to enforce that will be cited as the cause of project failure. Harry's position is untenable, but he appears to have little option but to continue to play the Enforcer role until he gets removed from the project and perhaps sacked.

A fundamental problem is that although Enforcers claim credit for their heroic rescues, their impact is largely restraining. The difficulties we have seen here are rooted in matters of energy. If there is energy, then Enforcers can attempt to channel it, and if all goes well, channel it into producing something of value. But Enforcers are not the generators of that essential energy; the projects are driven by the energy of others.

Enforcers may in fact kill off some of that vital energy, as in Matthew's negative impact on creativity in his government IT project (although that matters little to him, because he still emerges as a strong manager).

In Keith's machine development project, the producers of the project's energy, the engineering managers, know their power and resist his attempts to channel their efforts until it suits them. It is they, and not his Head Office sponsor, who are in control, and it is they who will decide when he can play his (to them very minor) part in the performance.

On Harry's local government project there is no energy. He is applying his rudder of control in a boat that is barely moving, and will get nothing but discredit from his efforts.

There are many projects that are subject to these and similar problems. The political and organisational world generates projects, in an endless stream, that are problematic for the Enforcer's control. Despite that, Enforcers must still try to control them. For any undesirable consequences emerging from that contradiction, the struggling Enforcer is in danger of taking the blame. With so many bad projects around for which you must take responsibility, how can you play this role and still prosper? How can you escape personal disaster?

Well firstly, things will not be universally bad. Matthew, who closed down the creative efforts of the contributors, delivered a project that failed to provide the value his sponsors had wanted. And yet he was a great success! The sponsor, who did not want to advertise the deficiencies to his political masters, congratulated Matthew for his sterling efforts. Matthew moved on to manage (as an Enforcer) bigger and better projects. At the end of a project the overwhelming desire of sponsors and managers is to claim success. Enforcers should not be too pernickety about what was originally intended. If the result is that something 'good enough' is delivered by the project, reasonably on time, then success can be claimed and you should trumpet your achievement. Good reputations are often built on very flimsy foundations.

Secondly there are tactics that can protect you. If you apply your project management tools with care and precision you can ensure the blame for failings is well dispersed. You have not actually done the project work; you have not actually designed the ill-conceived facility or written the poorly-functioning software. If you have made any promises you have ensured they are clearly based on the promises of others, which you have carefully documented. When Harry's project comes to a standstill his local-government boss advises him to *"be rigorous on agreements and paperwork to protect your backside"*. There will always be another party you can point at, who did not meet their commitments.

Thirdly you can play for time. Sometimes you are put in charge of projects that are not really fit for the Enforcer's style, but if you persist, something may transpire. In the confusion some progress might be made, or the dynamics of power may change. Some part of the project will suddenly become fit for Enforcer action, and you will focus on that and claim your success.

These options are encouraging. Although you may find yourself in impossible situations there are tactics available that let you keep your head high and maintain your reputation. Even if these simple tactics misfire and you are left playing the role of scapegoat, the evidence in the stories of Enforcer shows them to be resilient. A manager labelled as 'failing' will often spend some months sidelined, but then return to the action and have another chance to find that nugget of success – all that is needed for rehabilitation as a strong controlling project manager.

An aside – making promises

I have now covered the essential tactics and life of the Enforcer, but the topic of promises, the giving and receiving of them, perhaps needs more attention.

A manager might pursue a policy of avoidance. The strategy is never to make a commitment unless its delivery is clearly possible, never to give those promises demanded by your own managers unless all uncertainties have been cleared and there are cast iron commitments from the project team and contractors. In this way you can protect your day-to-day position. But you will find this strategy has some problems. Firstly it demands analysis. How do you know that this will work? You will regress to being the Analyst, investigating everything and dropping nuggets of advice to your bosses who will make the decisions, and so diminishing your managerial standing. Secondly, your bosses and sponsors will get increasingly intolerant of your stance. They are under pressure themselves to make commitments, and your precious hovering around waiting for clarity will not appeal to them.

Machiavelli's advice to Princes is highly relevant. You will not scatter promises around without good reason, but when the situation demands a promise – for you to get the role you want and the power you need to do it – then the promise should be given. There is always leeway to claim success, to point out mitigating circumstances, to transfer the blame for your lack of good faith to more deserving people.

You should also be aware that others know this tactic. Your team and your contractors will be looking for those get-out clauses that let them make promises without any fear of the consequences if things go wrong. They too may be giving their promises lightly.

Is this a good place to be?

It is evident that the Enforcer archetype can be played with credit and reputation. Managers who are accomplished Enforcers (and proficient in claiming success) often move on upwards in their organisations. They take senior manager roles, and continue to perform in a similar style, bringing junior project managers into order. They often appear in public as experienced advisers and high-profile pundits, proclaiming the value of Project Management to the wider world. Politicians want their pet projects and are all too willing to use the standard enforcement rhetoric: others let the projects run out of control, but we will have proper Project Management. Our Enforcer, perhaps sniffing the prospect of a good job, willingly appears beside those politicians, talking tough management to back this line of argument.

That is a rewarding life for some, a satisfying position to

occupy on the grand project stage. The role can also be played at a lower level for many years, its performers avoiding bad spots when they can, claiming their reputations on partial successes, perhaps taking a knock on a particularly bad project but then picking themselves up and playing on.

But we must recognise it is a subservient role. The Enforcer is the lackey of someone in power, somebody's Enforcer, the strong-arm henchman. Without a powerful sponsor, the role is unplayable.

Enforcement is not always the winning strategy. The politics of projects sometimes open out and people will look for more creativity or more opportunity for creating value, and then they will not be satisfied with your claim that "the project has been delivered". They will expect something better than the sight of an Enforcer closing down options and constraining an endeavour that could have delivered much more.

You have the option, at that point, of rowing on against the tide. It will always turn and you will come out of the situation with your reputation intact. You will look steadfast, and can continue to pursue your chosen ambition.

But there are better moves than this. While our local-government project manager Harry is taking the blame for the inaction of his surrounding managers, and waiting for recovery and the restoration of his reputation, perhaps he has alternatives? He is aware of his past life as an Analyst, that Garden of Eden where people got together and decided what to do, and then did it. But that option lacks promise as a new destination, perhaps merely a dream that places the blame for his current misfortunes on today's management culture.

However an Enforcer in Harry's situation also has the option of moving forwards, towards becoming the person who really knows what is best to do. How could vision or energy be brought into this constipated managerial world? Perhaps space could be created, unpressurised, where people could reflect on what is really going on and find a new sense of direction. Perhaps our manager could 'get a grip' by taking a more independent line. There are career journeys one can take beyond the territory of mere enforcement of project processes.

There will always be those among you who think the

Enforcer role is 'real' project management, who know how to deal in firm commitments and enforcing them, who fancy yourselves as tough-guy managers.

For the rest of us, less convinced of the Enforcer's vision of the project world, it is better to look for those more creative possibilities.

6. PLAYING THE EXPERT

Knowing what to do

We now come to the Expert mode of playing the role of project manager. The basic claim of the Expert is simply this: I know this stuff so do as I say.

There are of course all manner of 'experts', in varied disciplines, engaged in project work, who are not, and will never be, project managers. The archetype of the (capitalised) Expert is not this person in a subsidiary role, but one who has taken control of the project – a decision-making project manager – and is running it according to the principles of their specialised discipline.

I should perhaps first apologise to some readers because this chapter may be something of a diversion. In the previous two chapters I recommended, to those who play the Analyst or the Enforcer, that they might move on and develop new strategies, new directions, for their managerial careers. Those who are hoping to take that advice are unlikely to find the archetype I now present an attractive option. It is hard to become an Expert, and once there it takes your career along a path that may be rewarding, but is narrowly channelled.

However I suggest that those with no intention of becoming an Expert should read the chapter anyhow. Many of the problems the other archetypes confront on their projects arise from the presence of expert workers and managers. An understanding of their ways of thinking and performing may provide some enlightenment as to why more generalist managers often find these people so insufferably difficult.

The professional institutions of Project Management like to throw doubt on the validity of this Expert mode of operation. Their line of argument is that to manage a project you only need the tools and capabilities of Project Management; knowledge of particular skilled disciplines is not necessary; you can manage anything. We have seen our Analysts try this by immersing themselves in the team and the project work, seeking to understand everything that's going on. We have seen Enforcers try to deal with experts by getting commitments from them and holding them to their promises. Neither of these approaches to controlling experts fares particularly well.

The simple fact, uncomfortable for the priests of Project Management, is that experts in particular knowledge disciplines have immense powers in the project field, and often have the capability to act as the de facto project manager – the Expert. These people have taken years to develop their understanding of their discipline. To them the 'profession' of project management looks decidedly lightweight. Many discipline experts can readily exploit this weakness to their personal advantage. The norms of their own specialist discipline can trump the rules and practices laid down by mere Project Managers.

We find Expert project managers in a wide range of business and public sectors. The four examples I will use here to describe the Expert performance concern:

> Thomas, who works in the oil industry, is project manager for a safety upgrade of an industrial facility. It is an environment of advanced engineering technology and extensive regulation.

> Chris, who works for a business and financial consultant, is project manager for an assessment carried out on behalf of a corporate client looking for a larger company to buy them out.

Simon, who works in IT for a government department, is manager for a roll-out of computer and software upgrades in far-flung local offices.

Louise, who is a psychologist, is manager for a human resources project for a health service institution, to identify clinical specialists to be trained as health service managers, and to design their development programme.

These areas of work are diverse but all highly tangible as formal projects. We are not wandering off into some less-than-a-project zone of working. There are clearly specified requirements, a project team to be managed, defined deliverables, and a laid-out programme of work. The jobs in hand need to be managed as projects, but their leaders are not I-can-do-anything project managers; they are people with thorough knowledge of the specific subject matter that underpins the work.

The Expert brings a professional credibility to the role based on knowledge, experience and qualifications. Experts understand their profession as giving them an authoritative voice in a distinct zone of operation, and are persuasive about its value to the world. This is understandable since their personal credibility, their identity as an expert, is wholly dependent on that social value. They therefore proceed on the assumption that the world needs them.

The examples I am presenting here have an air about them of the external consultant, delivering a specialism to an organisation that lacks it. The projects are about organisation change, and the Expert project manager acts as a change agent, bringing new specialised thinking into an environment where it is novel. This is invariably a challenge. For example Thomas, in the oil industry, faces an uneven understanding within the client's organisation. Those who have set up the project and appointed him appreciate his knowledge, but there are others, with the capacity to damage the project quite seriously, who have a different agenda, and need to be brought back on-script.

This atmosphere of being an outside consultant generates a framing narrative of The Good Manager. Our Experts must present themselves as highly responsible, as trusted professionals, as guiding the team – both the project team and those within the client's organisation – in following the expert practices they bring to the job. They display an over-riding duty of care. On discovering a problem, Simon reports that:

> *My first priority was to placate the senior management and get to the bottom of the problems so that we could start to resolve them. Once we realised what had happened, I arranged for two of my best engineers to attend site and work through all of the problems and restore the user profiles and restore access to data.*

His first duty is to look after those in the client organisation.

Chris, who is away on holiday at a crucial project stage, comments on how he must handle this absence:

> *Every good manager knows that delegation is a key part of the role. However there is a significant difference between delegating whilst still being in control and delegation of entire control. This case was the latter. I would not be managing the transaction from [abroad] (though could not resist the temptation to follow the update [online]). I would still be at the end of the phone should I be required, but was trusting my team to conclude the assignment without me.*

This is a finely judged position on the nature of delegation. He takes the necessary action to delegate so his well-trained, well-instructed team can do the job while he is away. But even while acting as trusting with his team he feels an obligation, from his duty of care, to keep his eye on the proceedings from a distance.

So the overall picture is of a consultant, bringing a specialist team and directing a project that will deliver change within an organisation. This archetype reverses the standard assumption of the project management profession, that the generalist Project Manager will hold the reins and the whip, and use these to direct the subordinate experts working on their project. A survey of real project life shows that very often it is the expert who holds the reins (perhaps employing a project manager administrator to do the donkey work). In this mode they become the Expert archetype of project manager.

The performing Expert

For anyone wishing to perform as an Expert, the essential question concerns how to grasp that control, and so avoid being subservient to those ignorant Project Managers.

The big issue is the matter of legitimacy, intellectual weight and credibility. This is firstly a personal attribute. As Thomas says of his oil industry client:

> *Fortunately I am a high-credibility individual within this scenario, because that organisation, the client organisation, knows me personally very well, and my capability to make things happen.*

He is fortunate indeed, to have such a client, who can recognise the importance of his presence in the driving seat of the project. However the skill of the driver is only as good as the vehicle he is driving. Experts also make much of the processes of their profession. They promote their standard ways of doing the job, and stress how robust this process is, and its foundation in rigour, structure, objectivity and science. Louise is a good psychologist, but to operate with authority in the bureaucratic world of the health service she needs to bring a way of working that has a higher authority, beyond her own personal judgement. The Experts locate themselves, and their process, securely within the wider world of their profession, so their service to the project has the aura of being systematic and accredited in their wider professional community. For Louise this authority rests in the assessment methods of occupational psychology:

> *We had a very rigorous highly credible assessment process which the candidates went through.*

For Chris on the other hand, his authority rests within his organisation, the expert financial consultancy for whom he works, who claim vast experience and hence special expert knowledge of how such work as his must be carried out:

> *Every sale and purchase transaction has a standard process that takes place.*

Our Experts thus present themselves as the leader of expert team, perhaps delegating within that team but also placing themselves central to the project and its decisions. They act as the fount of knowledge, but also as the representative of a wider community, a rigorous and science-based professional group. They apply this knowledge thoroughly and systematically through the project life. Their strength is at the same time both personal and collective. In their field of work they will inevitably carry the day in the event of dispute with anyone less expert who might try to get in their way.

Experts can usually be found talking. Their position depends on their way of thinking pervading the project, and they must always be on hand to explain, and correct any deviation. Their rhetoric often employs variants of the contrast between competence and incompetence.

Take the matter of credibility, as described by Thomas:

Now on the contractor's side ... we had some very high credibility individuals in terms of long and excellent track records in doing this sort of thing and projecting this sort of thing ... And the programmes in principle were well understood on the other side.

Then [the client] appointed their HSE manager as the project manager from their side on the job, and that then takes us straight away to some challenge, because this guy was high credibility within his sphere – a bright guy – a first from a good university and so on. However he had no ... understanding of projects and how they worked ... and also he had no understanding of technical safety cases, because he had been purely involved in occupational safety. So the project ... immediately ran into treacle.

So Thomas not only claims the competence of his team and their knowledge of what is to be done, but does so at the expense of another discipline. That other person may be bright and have been to the right university, but that is not enough. To be in the wrong discipline, however close it may be to that of Thomas and his team, is sufficient cause to be discredited.

The rhetorical duality may also be stated in terms of the contrast between being rigorous or loose. Simon has a process for IT roll-out, and his manager may well understand it, but the manager is also playing another game and gets distracted from the true path:

> My manager (trying to win some brownie points) had decided that he would 'manage' this activity as it was high-risk, particularly for customer relations.
>
> We later found out that he hadn't actually confirmed that they were all logged out, and a number of them had still been using the system when the data migration started.
>
> Inevitably, this led to a number of problems with access, data loss etc.

Ultimately, whatever the cause, the unreliable people go off track and the necessary correction must be made. The Expert speaks of the situation in terms that make the deviation unacceptable, and remedial action is then taken. As Thomas later observes, action had to be taken *"so that we could get back to the script"*.

There are no half measures. The players in these project performances are either on-script or they are off-script, and if any player is the latter, the Expert will bring them back to the script, or get them moved out of earshot.

Experts know about the tools of project management. They are conducting a systematic operation, and good project administration is a necessary part of being organised. However they will use the minimum to keep track of what's done and what's yet to be done. They may employ a project administrator for this (and even call that person the 'Project Manager' while being clear they will be given daily instruction on what to do). For the Expert these duties are trivial, a mere clerical job. The heart of their toolkit is the process of their own specialist profession and its step-by-step application to the current project.

This professional presence is a very personal thing. Our Experts' value is embodied in the self. It is their physical presence on the project stage, representing their profession, personally ensuring that everyone knows what to do, that is the manifestation of their authority. They are not disposed to produce detailed documented procedures and standards. They leave that sort of thing to lesser disciplines, such as project management.

Inner life: being wanted

Our four examples all concern people who have been accepted and become the voice of authority on their project. However we should not forget Louise's earlier attempt to be an Expert (chapter 2) when she spoke good expert sense to her colleagues, but was ignored. There are many would-be Experts outside the project tent, offering themselves for sale to project buyers, but not being heard.

As Experts running projects this fear of becoming outsiders again colours our life at the helm. Even while in full project flow we can experience a continuing vulnerability. Our reputation is on display, and we are being judged. We have to work at all times to maintain our legitimacy, because it is always exposed to query. The sense of vulnerability is enhanced by a feeling of isolation, of having the sole responsibility for holding together the expert discipline and ensuring its rigorous application. Vigilance and persistence are essential to deal with problems that might undermine us: people off script, clients lacking interest, non-believers in the team, obstinacy of those with alternative and competing forms of expert knowledge.

Although nominally in charge, Louise has continuing problems making herself heard:

> So then we'd get messages from the Board who were making decisions without any expert input. So I tried to approach the Director concerned and he refused to take my calls.

> And then the message came down from above that it may not just be the top performing [people] who are allocated places [on the management development scheme]. The Board want to sign off, which was great; I wanted the Board's approval and agreement.

> So we went and we made a presentation to the Board, which I was able to attend and it was just so apparent to me that the Board didn't have a clue what they were doing.

And so she eventually gets that vital opportunity, to be heard, and to bring the Directors back into line with her Expert plans.

However Thomas's problems with the off-script manager in

his oil-industry client organisation go on and on:

> *He never actually understood, and asked for more presentations, and more written stuff about what the methodology was and how it was going to work and so on, and still refused to be convinced.*

This obstinate dissenter, struggling to handle Thomas's continuing onslaught of expert advice, eventually tries a different tactic and brings in another consultant to advise him. Fortunately for Thomas, this new advisor belongs to the same expert discipline family:

> *and they could suggest very little ... effectively they thought it was fine*

So that obstacle has been overcome, but the situation gets no better. After several months of struggle Thomas is driven to make a written intervention to the client's senior managers:

> *... I stoked it up by writing an articulation of the difficulties we were having, which summarised the difficulties.*
>
> *Now they would have heard those difficulties internally. They would have been transmitted through the technical community and the supervisory community. The senior management ... were aware that there was possibly something amiss, possibly an issue but not ready to move on it.*

And in the end this tactic, of presenting a formal 'articulation', generates the action Thomas wants; the difficult manager is removed from the project. Persistence has paid off. The Expert is back in control.

Success can actually attract more responsibility. People can load it on you, and you can't refuse without devaluing your profession. Louise is the project manager, but is dragged in to carrying out duties that were originally intended to be performed by the health service Human Resources department.

> *So what they asked me ... what they offered everybody who didn't get on to the programme but wanted to, a one-to-one with me, [which] was what they decided. They felt they couldn't handle it internally ...*

The claim of bringing personal value, embodied in your self, has responsibilities attached to it. It is difficult to back away from extra demands.

Because the position is so personal, the possible impact of being absent must be addressed carefully. If you could just be away for a time, with no consequence to the project, your importance would be seriously diminished, and your central position as valued servant could be lost. We saw Simon's problems earlier, when his less-than-expert manager took over for the IT upgrade at the distant government office.

Chris uses his absence (on holiday) to reinforce his expert position. We saw him delegating responsibility to his team for this absence, but he has taken steps to instruct them in detail before he departs, so that:

> ... my colleagues in the team knew what they needed to do and the issues that were unresolved; all parties knew what the next steps were to complete the transaction

Thus a possible hazard to his Expert position is transformed, through this story, into an enhancement, the giving of instructions being a clear demonstration of his value. We should note in passing that he doesn't leave a list of instructions. That would reduce his knowledge to something that can be encapsulated in a written procedure, hardly fitting for an Expert.

Being an Expert – a life

The stories told by Experts are about how they brought people into line with their Expert professional process: clients who didn't understand, clients whose organisations were ignorant of their discipline and had to learn, and individuals, usually other managers, who weren't competent in the discipline and had to be removed from the project.

These stories all display the Experts' immense sense of their value and relevance, and this is what makes them special. Their only need is for clients who are listening: who can be persuaded that standard project management isn't sufficient, and that an Expert is the person to lead their projects. They act in opposition to the standard project model in which a Project Manager is in charge, controlling the expert contributors. The Expert stories don't even admit to the possibility that they might work under such a regime.

From a project or client perspective we might have some criticisms to make of Experts. The fact that they are rather preachy can be wearing. At any hint of a deviation they will be there, whispering in our ear to bring us back to the right path. Their obsession with keeping us on track is rather restrictive. A single track tends to lead to a single destination. Perhaps we might like to go somewhere else. The project under Expert control can tend to take on a single form – the project formulated as the expert discipline would have it be.

I have suggested to Analysts and Enforcers that they might consider other options for how they play the project manager. I feel I would be insulting an Expert if I put forward such a proposition. Experts have invested their career identities in a single mode of existence. They want to be useful, and have developed an expertise so they may offer something of value to the world. So long as there are are people willing to listen to them, they will be reluctant to let go of that value, to become something else. At those moments of fluidity, when a project challenge might offer another possibility, a move in a different direction, the safe option is to stay in role.

When Experts stop being project managers, they go on being experts. It is a whole-life position, often carried through into retirement, when they continue to present their knowledge at conferences and hope for those little consultancy assignments that may bring in some cash and, more importantly, revalidate their status.

Being an Expert is not a life I would personally choose. It is too one-dimensional for my taste, and carries more than a hint of imprisonment. It is a prison of choice, but a constraint nonetheless. The Expert's way of thinking has been formed, and then frozen.

Regardless of that, I must express my admiration for Experts. They are a valuable and committed set of people and, moreover, a mischievous thorn in the flesh of conventional Project Management.

7. PLAYING THE IMPRESARIO

The Impresario – putting on a show

The essence of the Impresario mode of management is about doing something special. Its performer focuses attention on an amazing outcome: a rewarding event, or an object of great appeal.

We can immediately contrast this perspective with the thinking of the three archetypes we have looked at so far. If we were to ask an Analyst, an Enforcer or an Expert to tell us why their job was worthwhile they would respond in terms of themselves and their managerial abilities. Their role is to support a project which is essentially owned, in terms of its ambitions, by someone else. That is why I have suggested that those modes of working are essentially servile; the purpose of being a manager is to serve somebody else's agenda, and the individual's sense of worth is bound up in how well he or she fulfils that service. In contrast Impresarios claim their worth in terms of their contribution to something wonderful, their desire to be seen as people who have an impact.

The social and political world in which they operate invariably places difficulties in their way, and these must be overcome. In tackling such difficulties Impresarios have little commitment to any particular process. Times of crisis demand creative ideas: freestyle thinking where anything can be considered. The aim is to get from A to B, and the route is immaterial. There may be rules, but it is sometimes necessary to break those rules for the higher cause, that special outcome.

Impresarios are not normally specialists or experts, and so cannot achieve their aims on their own. They are highly dependent on the support of others. They must enthuse others to support that valued objective, become the leader of the cohort, the band of brothers (and sisters), in this together, carrying the project through.

The framing narrative of Impresarios is thus made up of three interlinked strands of thinking: their central driving mission, their flexible freethinking approach to problems, and their dependency on loyal supporters.

This way of working can be a way of life in some fields, for example arts projects or journalism. I will exemplify this briefly using the example of Conrad, who is organising a concert tour for young pianists.

Some readers might think themselves remote from that field of the arts, and may think this way of managing is not too relevant to their own position. However the style is also evident, as a break-out mode, across the project field, including the most hardware-orientated organisation-embedded projects. There are people working in rule-based organisations running 'private' projects out of the view of their senior managers. There are others who, at times of trouble, can take up the mantle of the Impresario, distance themselves from the prevailing management culture and liberate their work from the rigidity that surrounds them.

When this can be done, and how? We will examine these questions taking a close look at the story told by Frankie as she manages a project to put custom-built screens into a theatre. We will follow her activities as the screens are installed in the theatre during the course of one Saturday in December.

The Impresario's performance

The Impresario's principal rhetoric concerns the production of that 'desired object': what it is that will emerge from this brilliant project, and what we will need to do to attain it. For Conrad, that higher aim is the development of the young pianists:

> ... the experiences of meeting important international musicians and teachers, of performing overseas and of hearing overseas musicians performing ...

For Frankie, her troublesome project is:

> ... part of something that is really amazing ... theatres and screens ... a great feat ... pretty impressive.

When their aims are in danger of being thwarted, Impresarios lead the decision-making, interrogating the nature of the situation and asking what is possible. When things get difficult they use a rhetorical duality that contrasts the beaten track, and the expectation we should follow it, with break-out, and the possibility of adopting strategies that are non-standard and creative. When Frankie's screens are delivered the installers don't have the right lifting equipment with them. She doesn't wait; there are enough people around to carry the boxes:

> *So the installers are taking stuff down, but they don't have the equipment to roll 1500lbs of equipment out. So we had to do that. So human beings, people, about twelve of us, carrying boxes and laying them on top of pick-up trucks. And the quickest way to get from point A to point B was to go across the lawn, instead of going all the way round through the traffic. At the end of the project the ground-keeper yelled at me because I rolled over his lawn ... the last thing I was worried about. The question was what can be sacrificed?*

So the beaten track – along the road through the traffic – has been abandoned in favour of the unprepared, the direct route across the lawn. The lawn, and in principle anything else in the way, can be sacrificed for that project objective.

Conrad's concert tour similarly faces several potential show-stoppers, but these are tackled with a side-stepping manoeuvre. If the plan isn't working, we'll try something else. A last minute shortage of funding is rectified when:

> *one of my golfing friends, who had heard these young*

> *musicians, told me that a bequest from his wife's family would give [...] towards our venture ...*

Most seriously, during the concert tour, Conrad is knocked unconscious when he falls in an accident in a restaurant.

> *The next day, I returned to consciousness, but with broken tendons of the right arm and double vision. ...*

But his supporting team arrive at his hospital bedside, and plans for transport and administration are revised to keep the tour on the road while Conrad is immobile in his hospital bed.

This free-style manner, improvising to keep going, epitomises management by Impresarios. An obstacle appears, they query what can be done, they find a resolution, they re-plan, and they get everyone moving again. It is their creative energy that motivates the team and keeps the project rolling forward.

They are highly dependent on others for their achievements. For every flexible change of plan they are asking people to go beyond what has been previously agreed. When Frankie needs help to carry her screens across the lawn she just asks:

> *I went up to them and said "I really need your help. It'll be twenty minutes". And they said "Sure, no problem".*

We managers can only do this if we have already established strong long-term working relationships. Help with carrying may be a fairly mundane request, but often we will be approaching gifted people and asking them to go beyond their normal obligations.

Frankie's worst problem arises when it is discovered that the delivered screens are too big to fit in their space in the theatre. She checks and re-checks the measurements, but realises something has to be done. She brings everyone together. Nobody there on the day has formal responsibility for resolving this problem, but they discuss it, as Frankie says *"free of any constraints"*, and decide to cut the screen. The electrician on site has a suitable saw, and he does the job. This act is well beyond his remit, but he does it.

At this point Frankie's project is in uncharted territory. It has broken away from the norms and rules of standard project management. In such circumstances, as the moralisers will tell us, transgression must have a cost. There will be consequences! Obviously we cannot just ignore such consequences. These inventive decisions need some thought. Frankie and her team go through the issues: the effect on the design, the warranty, the absence of approval, the view of the fire marshal (*"Is there a fire marshal coming round today?"*), security, the attitude of the unions, what their bosses might think, etc. However the implications of their chosen course are not obvious or documented, nor have they been subject to a review by knowledgeable people; they are difficult judgements, made in haste, in the heat of the moment.

But the likely consequences are discussed openly, Frankie takes the lead, and the decision is taken; the electrician cuts the screen, and the project moves on.

In taking this decision and acting on it, there is more than a hint of a secret society, the little conspiratorial band, and that sense of complicity, of being 'in it together', which binds them and reinforces their commitment to what they are doing, and of being collectively willing to transgress.

Frankie's band of supporters is tight-knit, but this is not the norm. It is a result of the circumstances of her particular crisis: the urgency, the people who are there at the theatre that morning. Most Impresario players have the time and the social network to cast their nets more widely for collaborators. Conrad, as we have seen, gets help from the family of a golfing friend. There are many other examples. Phil, who is running an undercover project for his group in an engineering company, needs some software development and persuades a colleague to do this *"in the gaps"* of his overt work for the company. Isabel is managing the production of a publication and finds that her intended artwork is covered by a copyright, so commissions new artwork from a friend who is a retired art school lecturer.

Why are people so helpful, doing these things for us? The truth, ignored by those embedded in the tidy project management world of contracts and resource plans, is that people like to be useful. The 'helpful person' identity is good to have. That desired object, the goal of the project, can attract supporters from all directions, people who want to contribute to the social good promised by our Impresario.

I have highlighted the free-style nature of the Impresario's approach to strategies and resources, but this is not to suggest that the approach is in any way casual. The hard-nosed tools of project management are actually crucial to this performance. Conrad has a detailed schedule for the concert tour, backed up with contracts. When Frankie's suppliers deliver the screens but fail to bring the equipment needed to install them she can immediately point to their obligations:

> *I had to show them the pieces of paper – thank goodness for contracts. "You see this part where it says 'supplier to install all equipment, scaffolding' ... that's you!"*

Frankie unleashes her inner Enforcer. The supplier (who had already failed to meet an obligation to move the equipment into the building) comes, belatedly, into line with the contract.

Flexible thinking and improvisation central to the Impresario performance, but are only viable if they are backed by careful preparation.

Inner life: is this really going to work?

The sense of mission that makes this mode of management attractive also brings the seeds of its vulnerability. Presenting yourself as the manager, so committed to the objective, puts you on the spot. If things start to go wrong, you will be put through the mill.

Conrad's financial crisis shows this up. When his initial fundraising efforts have failed to collect sufficient funds for the tour his personal inclination is to abort the plan. It is too hazardous. However expectations have been generated, the young pianists have prepared and are ready to go. He raised everyone's hopes, and a cancellation would let them down. A vision created and promoted cannot be abandoned lightly. The funding crisis places an obligation on Conrad to solve it. In this way the Impresario manager becomes a slave to the objective, being driven along by the mission and the collective energy it has generated.

To be in this position is not always a happy experience. Our earlier archetypes, the Analyst, the Enforcer, the Expert, love crises and the cut and thrust of argument. They relish opportunities to wade in to controversy, and to set others right. It is the crises make them the people they are. Impresarios, on the other hand, just want to get there, to those magical objects that will be the outcomes of their projects. The obstacles and setbacks that threaten that outcome can distress them. They fear they might not make it to their destination, which would be disastrous. Their transgressions can make them uncomfortable. When her project is facing its worst problems Frankie exudes outward confidence as she makes the critical decisions, but her inner world is in turmoil:

> *It was the worst project of my life. Something went wrong every 30 minutes: another disaster, and another disaster.*

Note that this fear is bound up only with the core project, not with any other social consequences. The theatre ground-keeper, for example, was very upset about the damage done to his lawn, but who cares if the project was kept moving? These upsets are mere side shows.

On the positive side, the Impresario archetype can be quite satisfying for many, in the sense of freedom and creativity it can bring. We can tell ourselves that we are free spirits, and it is others who are bound by management rules and conventions. This is good, but the reality of free-style action is not as liberated as we might wish. Our actions are still very much socially constrained in two ways. Firstly we are wholly dependent on others: those who are useful and will support us at our time of need. As leaders setting out into the unknown we are worthless unless someone is following us. We are always in their hands: they might let us down or abandon us when they think we are taking them a step too far. Secondly our off-the-beaten-track diversions may take us into dangerous territory. Frankie claimed her decision-making was *"free of any constraints"*, but then, having considered the possibilities, brought the discussion back to the real world, and set about analysing what those constraints might be. Furthermore there could be unexpected consequences; she could easily have misjudged the position and could end up in serious trouble.

A decision 'free of any constraints' is an illusion. There is no such thing as a go-it-alone project. All are socially embedded.

We are dependent on both sides: on those joining us to help, and on those around us whose aim is to hinder.

Our most serious fear, given our focus on achieving that desired end-point, is that we will simply take a wrong path. Frankie took her decision to saw a chunk off the screen in the course of a meeting where nobody present understood the design and the implications of what they were deciding. *"We don't know if it's going to get hot"* she observed. She was out of her depth, but had to continue regardless. In this sort of situation, exposed to risks of which we know little, we can easily become the agents of the collapse of our own free-wheeling identity.

Fears such as these can easily pull us into a secret world, hiding our decisions (or sometimes whole projects) from public gaze. People don't need to know what we actually did to achieve that great and admired goal. But on the other hand, as with any professional identity, we need recognition to pursue our standing, to create those professional faces by which the world may know us. We must tell our stories, to our peers if to nobody else, so we may be clearly recognised as creative decision-makers, the people with flair, on our project stages.

Who can play Impresario?

The Impresario mode can be an attractive proposition, bringing a sense of real achievement and also the possibility of a break-out from the rigidity of the previous archetypes. Instead of being servants to our senior managers we are moving into a zone of creative action, even if we are never fully free of wider constraints, or from the fear that our free-style strategies may take us into trouble.

Some lucky people, such as Conrad, have found a sphere of operation where this style of working can be the norm. But what are the possibilities for the rest of us, embedded in our organisations, in the corporate world or in public-sector projects?

To consider this question, we must return to the basics of professional identity. The creation of our self, the person we might become, lies in those moments of fluidity. At such a moment a crisis has thrust us into unfamiliar territory. We must assert an identity that gives us the authority to make sense of the situation, and to propose a course of action and pursue it. Frankie is taking a short break when such a moment arrives:

> ... 10 minutes after I'd sat down, the installer came to me and said "your screens are too big", and I think my heart stopped.

Until this moment she has been operating essentially in Enforcer mode (with a minor trespass across that lawn). What are her options how? Her decision could well determine the course of her managerial life. At this juncture, who can she become?

This is not an easy question to penetrate. If we interview her after the event we will find that she has adopted her new-found identity and will speak to reinforce it. The question "what were your options?" will inevitably get the reply "I had no alternative." However we can stand back and look at her story as outsiders, and ask ourselves whether there were other possibilities. What might those have been?

Concerning the choice she actually made, we should note the importance of the context that enabled it. At the moment she needed them she was surrounded by useful people, and one of them in particular was carrying the implement (the saw) she needed to pursue her new strategy. The path she chose, the Impresario route, would not have been available to her without the support of others.

We should also note her sense of purpose, her admiration for the object she is delivering to her client. This drives her preference to push ahead, breaking rules if necessary. The other possibilities are unattractive because they betray that cause. Her commitment appears to be a prerequisite for her chosen course. But on the other hand, we might argue that perhaps her belief in the product is part of her new performance, a story about herself and her commitment that she constructs to justify the moves she is going to make. Whatever the timing however, whether her admiration for the product precedes or coincides with the emergence of the new Frankie, it is an essential part of her new performance.

Alternatively, instead of making that end-product her foremost concern, could she have re-iterated her belief in the order and controls of project management? Could she have continued in her Enforcer role, getting managers out of their beds if necessary, and demanding compliance? She refutes this possibility:

> ... it's 12 o'clock on a Saturday the week before Christmas, who's around? But no one's around. And these screens were custom ordered, so who is going to fix it?

A committed Enforcer would not waver at this point. He or she would make sure that the responsibility remained firmly with the supplier, exactly where the project plan had put it. An Enforcer does not even contemplate a course of action that relieves others of their contractual obligations. If the job goes wrong (as well it may) then it will be the supplier who is at fault. If the supplier fails to respond to the crisis and the project flops, there will be retribution. No doubt Frankie too would be in trouble, and probably get moved off the job. However we saw in our discussion of Enforcers that this cycle of reputation is quite normal, part of the archetypal life. Others would have continued as an Enforcer. Frankie could reasonably have done so.

Immediately after the crisis situation has arisen, Frankie, unsettled by her feeling of dissatisfaction with the Enforcer option, starts to act like an Analyst. She assembles her team and immerses herself in the expertise they can provide. Her moment of choice, when she could have continued in this mode, came when she could have presented her analysis of the situation to her boss, and awaited his judgement. However her boss has previously told her clearly that he does not think highly of project managers who hand their decisions to him. This would obviously be a career-limiting move, and she rejects it. But it is nonetheless, again, a course that many would follow at this juncture.

The option to be Expert is not available to her, gone before the moment of crisis arrives. Frankie might have chosen earlier to become expert in the technology, but she didn't. She might also have delegated the management of the installation to an appropriate Expert, who would have specialised knowledge of what to do, but again the fact is she didn't. At her moment of fluidity, these possibilities weren't available to her.

In summary, in wishing to continue as a project manager her

viable alternatives for action were either to demand compliance from the supplier (Enforcer), or else pass the decision upwards (Analyst). Either was possible, but either would take Frankie along a severely limited career path.

Her decision, then, was to take a calculated risk, to adopt the persona that would take towards a more dynamic career. The alternatives she rejected would channel her career towards a low-status future. The conditions she needed to launch her new identity, the amazing product, the useful people, were to hand at the moment of choice. These factors created an opportunity, and she took it. Those present, complicit in her strategy, ratified her identity as a creative rule-breaking manager.

In introducing the concept of archetypes I was at pains to make it clear that these are not rigid species. We can change, and adopt a new archetype to deal with a new challenge. However in practice people playing the archetypes I introduced earlier have a tendency to remain in character. They have found a way of being a manager that suits them, and they prefer to cling to that mode unless it becomes entirely dysfunctional.

I am aware that the detailed analysis I have presented here, of one person's story related some time after the events, is speculative. However I believe it reveals important principles about the nature of the choices managers can make. The statement "I had no alternative" carries with it the shadow of an unstated sub-clause, which is "given the person I want to be".

The story also demonstrates that the Impresario model is there for all to try. For some, becoming an Impresario manager may be a fairly obvious career path. They find themselves at the head of a creative project, uncluttered by managerial norms and restrictive rules in their own organisation, and having reasonable flexibility of strategy and action.

Those of us submerged in more institutionalised endeavours should not be disheartened. This way of managing is often also to be found lurking in the recesses: those projects kept hidden from higher management, and those occasions when unreasonable impediments can be overcome through some unapproved creative actions. Difficult times, when things go wrong, can be taxing for managers, but they are opportunities for us to become more flexible in our strategies: to take a risk, to cut a corner, to break some rules, to ask some favours. Some of us may be driven in this free-style direction by our passion for the value in the project's objectives. Others can still take this new direction lacking such a commitment, but we must acquire it quickly, because that notion, that we are delivering something special and valuable, is the essence of our Impresario's story, driving the performance we put on when up against the odds.

For those of you who suffer under the weight of institutional norms, playing Impresario could be a rewarding way to lighten your burden. It will also enhance your sense of pride, that you are having a positive impact on the wider world, and not acting merely as the slave of your bosses and their dismal management systems.

8. PLAYING THE MASTER OF CEREMONIES

Projects as a social practice

With the Impresario archetype we saw the significance of 'value' as a resource that can energise a project manager's performance. By focusing attention on a valued end point the Impresario drives action in the direction of his or her choosing, and emerges as a creative and decisive manager. However our examples for that archetype were remarkably free of any dispute about what 'value' might actually be. Our performers were free to define, and demand allegiance to, a singular objective, and dismiss as trivial any dissenting notions of value put forward by those on the peripheries of their projects.

There is however an alternative, embodied in the Master of Ceremonies mode of managing, which is to acknowledge that ideas about what constitutes 'value' can be diverse, and yet still incorporated into a project strategy. For example, we saw Frankie, an Impresario, ride roughshod over the ground-keeper's lawn to get her equipment into the building. A Master of Ceremonies would be loath to behave like that, and would prefer to ask how the needs of the ground-keeper might be brought within the ambit of the project. This is a difficult question; we shall see that Master of Ceremonies is a difficult archetype to play.

Those at the forefront of the project management profession have recognised value as important, but their inclination is to start at the top. Someone with political power defines a purpose, in terms of a desired social outcome, and follows this by defining a project, its deliverables and objectives, that is to produce this outcome. The project manager is then employed to deliver the project of defined scope, while at the same time keeping an eye on the social purpose that gave birth to it. This does not come naturally; we can note that our more conventional managers, the Enforcers and Analysts, showed little interest in what the overall social purpose of their projects might be. In contrast, the Master of Ceremonies argues that notions of value and purpose should not be defined from the top, but should be socially inclusive.

For our main example, Ryan, who works in local government, has the apparently simple responsibility of building children's playgrounds. Many would think that you just build something and leave them to it. However the situation is fraught with political tensions:

> ... *with officers threatened with the sack, accusations of racism, nimbyism and inter-generational tensions.*

We will also consider the managerial performance of Stewart, who is employed by a charitable organisation to manage recycling projects. For this charity the *"overriding aims are social"*; their basic purpose is to support people with diverse needs.

Thirdly we will hear the thoughts of Bernard, who finds the Master of Ceremonies mode of working a useful, but temporary, approach for his projects in the aerospace industry.

For Masters of Ceremonies, their philosophy of project management is about creating space: zones where people with diverse aims can come together. Through interaction they will discover areas of commonality, which will become invested in the project. Hence ideas of what constitutes 'value', in their multiplicity, become realised through the single project. This does not become an open agenda. Our managers, agents of their organisations, have a topic of focus, which determines what the project will be about. For Ryan, for example, it is about children and recreation; for Stewart it is about recycling.

What goes on within those broad definitions of scope is, however, up for negotiation. Their project scopes are free-style, open, organic, and developed in the absence of an imposed policy framework from above. For his playground project, Ryan is explicitly aware of the:

> *unbounded nature of the rules applying ... in regeneration projects*

The challenge is to resolve the competing aims and possibilities in a way that is creative.

At the core of the Master of Ceremonies' mode of operation is a rejection of short-termism. They see everywhere conventional projects that get defined, constrained and completed by their managers, but don't actually deliver their potential value. They blame this prevalence of poorly performing projects on the obsession with targets, controls and the simple rationalities of planning and doing. They reject the thinking that elsewhere makes people into Enforcers and Analysts.

They reject these norms, and yet they must act effectively as managers. I have not chosen to call these people the Hosts (or the Hostesses) of projects. They are not running open houses. The term 'Master of Ceremonies' is appropriate because they are masters (ie those in control) of the ceremonies that comprise the social processes of projects. To resist the normal political pressures on projects, which work to close down options (and employ Enforcers as their willing agents), the Masters of Ceremonies must create instead robust processes that work to open up possibilities, creating that much needed space: the leeway in which people with varied interests can come together, and in which alternatives can be brought from the wings to take centre stage.

In this way Masters of Ceremonies are putting up a resistance to old-guard project management. But resistance itself is not sufficient. To oppose the old framing narratives of projects they need a new framing narrative of their own. This narrative proclaims a New Age in project management, in which society as a whole will at long last get good value from the projects it commissions.

The performance of the Master of Ceremonies

In the prevailing control-oriented project management culture, promises have been made, and those who have made them will push to see something done now: fast decisions, so that something can be made, and success can be claimed.

Those playing the Master of Ceremonies need to find a way to resist decisions under pressure, because they will not work out well. As Ryan puts it:

> *It's only with hindsight that we know that we have made a bad decision but we can often tell immediately when we are being forced to into a vacuum starved of time and space.*

The rejection of short-termism has to be more than our personal opinion. The rhetoric of resistance to it, which contrasts the illusions of that short-term gain with the substance of long-term value, must become part of our explicit performance.

That long-term value is found through consultation. Bernard observes that:

> *... the creation of a sound project is a very human process. You can follow procedures to the letter and still end up with a project that's doomed to fail.*

Masters of Ceremonies make use of various rhetorics of space. Stewart likes a horticultural metaphor (linking it to that short-term vs long-term duality):

> *You have to provide the space for ideas to take root and come to fruition. A focus on project deadlines does not encourage creativity, generate social capital or build cohesion: in fact it does the opposite.*

The creation of formal arrangements for discussion is critical for defending against short-term pressures, by giving voice to the wider community of people with a stake in the project. Concerning Ryan's project, the existing playground had:

> *... become the focus for misuse and was under-used by local people. Local Asian youths, growing up in an area with little play space, and backed by councillors wanted a football pitch on the play area. Other residents, mainly African Caribbean*

and second and third generation Irish wanted it to remain as a family playground, but made fit for purpose.

In the face of this contention Ryan seeks *"time to breathe"*. He acts to create space:

> *I attempted to gain some control and breathing space by setting my own timescales ... [and found] scope for alternative structures*

When the work to build the playground is about to go ahead, he hears that:

> *... the MP was concerned that a group of residents were going to block the scheme and that some council staff weren't 'on side'. Whilst attempting to provide assurances that this wasn't the case I proposed that an outside voluntary sector agency be brought in to undertake further local consultation. This helped to provide some breathing space to untangle the knot of competing interests and in particular to prevent direct confrontation between the two groups.*

For Bernard's aerospace projects he is very much aware of the need to resolve disagreements before moving onwards:

> *If some people are against some facet of the project their opposition will sap the project energy.*

His process is simple:

> *We have meetings galore; some weeks my diary contains nothing but wall-to-wall meetings.*

As a consequence, our projects are perpetually open to change. However we are not dealing with an entirely open agenda. There is no value created if we never complete the job. At this stage our inner Analyst will be called into play to help the onward movement. However we will expand the Analyst's concern with the knots of the technical complexities of the project, to include the untangling of knots in the project's environment, the complexities of its political world. We must hear all voices, but the project remains ours to design and plan. The need, above all, is to find a project agenda that will gain the support, and harness the energy, of all parties.

Although Bernard's *"meetings galore"* appear open-ended, they in fact serve his own purpose:

> You have to find their boundaries – what they can do and what they cannot possibly do – and understand how these limit their possible actions.

So the meetings provide a stage for the interested parties, but also serve to support his own analysis that will lead him to designing the 'right' project.

Stewart's flexibility of approach on his recycling projects extends to bringing outside parties into a collective responsibility for undertaking the project's tasks. This supports his aim of helping people in the widest sense:

> Relief of poverty, helping the disadvantaged, protecting the environment and providing employment experience for those who have difficulty finding jobs.

Ryan has a more conventional, in-house team, planning, and re-planning at every scope change, and organising the project delivery. They have to be protected. For example Ryan has told the politicians that the project will take 18 months, but has to keep them from questioning and pressurising his team (who know that the construction itself can be completed in 9 months). Otherwise that *"breathing space"* will be lost.

Not an easy act

The position of a Master of Ceremonies is delicate. At every difficult moment there are political pressures: to exclude the outsiders, take quick decisions, pin down the scope of the project and move to completion.

Experienced competent Masters of Ceremonies recognise when it is essential to stop and talk, and wrong to press on. They have to be alert to what is going on around the project, aware of the social forces that may later cause problems or make the project less effective in producing its desired social impact. When Ryan's MP raises concerns about a group who may move to oppose the project, Ryan needs to make his judgement. Is this real? Is their opposition justified? Or will they acquiesce if the project moves on without consulting them? The identity being performed is exhibited in difficult situations such as these. The Master of Ceremonies is the person who can say: "Stop. There is a new idea here, another agenda we can incorporate into our project that will enhance its value. We must open out the discussion". But who has such authority? Who must you become if you are going to be listened to when you resist those forces that are demanding that discussion should be closed?

We have noted that our principal defence against short-term thinking is in the possession of a process: that we have established and formalised a procedure to create that social stage on which we can resolve the diverse needs of different parties. However the authority to take such action lies in our person, not in our processes.

Central to the possession of that authority is the matter of trust. Those around us must be comfortable that they are in safe hands; that the pause we are proposing has a good purpose, will result in a better project, and will be resolved in a timely manner. A call to 'stop' must also be heard as a call to proceed, but in a more productive direction.

The trust placed in Stewart is evident. He has been granted free space within his charitable organisation, to take whatever time is needed to consult and negotiate, to create more effective, value-generating, projects. This is an unusual position.

For the rest of us our permission to play Master of Ceremonies will be hard-won. Ryan concentrates on gaining the trust of a powerful local-government director, who understands his process, and has been persuaded of the validity of his project philosophy. However I would think his chances of getting any general acceptance of his role are poor; his chosen mode of managing will be a matter of struggle and negotiation at every stage, of every project.

I have written about Masters of Ceremonies in a manner that I hope is sympathetic to them, and so I may have given the impression they are fighting against regressive or unreasonable opposition. But we have already met some of their opponents in previous chapters. We have heard the complaints about *"treacle"* and *"endless debate"* (which I will not detail again) from our Enforcers, Experts and Impresarios. To these people, Masters of Ceremonies can be infuriating. At moments when others would take decisions and act, they set up yet another committee and re-open debates others had closed long ago. Their reputations are not helped by their tendency to retreat, at critical moments, into generalisations about the philosophy of projects and management (quite evident in the examples I have given from their stories). It is not difficult to understand why they face perpetual opposition.

Towards something better

While the Master of Ceremonies has a difficult part to play, it provides its performer with a strong moral standing. A Master of Ceremonies has a sense of self-worth, of personal standing in a complex social world. Masters of Ceremonies know they are better people than the pen-pushers, control freaks and flunkies who they know populate much of the project management world.

Given it is a difficult option, could we consider the archetype as something occasional, or temporary? When we have had enough of working parties and committees we could close down the talking and revert to Enforcer mode. Even better, we could hand over, as Bernard does:

> *My job isn't like the book version, which is about project execution – administering projects that already exist. That's not a very interesting job as far as I'm concerned; someone else can do it. My job is to make projects – to get them up and running in a highly complex environment.*

So despite his acknowledgement of the *"highly complex environment"*, Bernard attempts a rhetorical sleight of hand, which divides the life of a project into two distinct and separate phases, that of making projects and that of executing them, the one following the other. (And those concerned with the former are, of course, superior beings to those concerned with the latter.)

From the project perspective, his argument is weak. Do those complex social processes suddenly come to an end when the project has been defined? Do the different parties, with their diverse agenda, just melt away? Where will Bernard be when late objections come in from people who think their interests have been misrepresented? Presumably he will have moved on elsewhere, making another project that someone else will have to complete.

Regardless of whether we intend to play it as a temporary or permanent role, the question remains of how we can become a Master of Ceremonies. It could take us many years to establish that authoritative free-ranging persona. Can we perhaps experiment with the role, to try it out?

To start out in this direction we would watch out for those moments when another party, with an alternative agenda, appears off-stage to our closed project. We can choose such a moment as our chance to stand up and say "stop – this isn't right". If you decide to try this tactic you will need two things to hand. The first is a convincing explanation of how this pause is going to lead to a better outcome. The second is a clear set of moves – meetings, committees, events – which you will use to bring the new party on stage. If you are prepared, then the appearance of that new party on the project scene might be your moment of fluidity, your opportunity to set out in a new direction.

However I think this would be a brave act. That moment of project crisis is likely to be fraught with political intrigues. Another archetype, articulating a sense of the situation in a way that shows an immediate way forward, is much more likely to carry the argument.

In fact, our example Masters of Ceremonies appear to have arrived in their authoritative positions before their projects started. Ryan's manner of arrival is hinted at in his comments about tensions at the beginning of this chapter (*"officers threatened with the sack, accusations of racism, nimbyism and inter-generational tensions"*). His political masters have been unable to resolve these tensions but have proceeded to set up the project despite the general turmoil. When faced with messy, intractable disputes, what could be easier for them than to pass the problem to Ryan, for him to resolve during the project? He has attained his identity as holder of the complex dispute before he has become the project manager.

The best route of entry for those aspiring to become a Master of Ceremonies is therefore through putting yourself forward as a general mediator, and later becoming project manager with your mediator hat already on your head, your persona established and accepted. You may then find the authority to speak as mediator, and play Master of Ceremonies, as your project progresses.

Those who get to play the part of Master of Ceremonies immerse themselves in its way of thinking. They are dismayed by the decrepit world of orthodox project management, which they see as a sordid game: inventing senseless targets and then meeting them, forever claiming credit for successful completion of projects that are socially worthless. Masters of Ceremonies have a conviction that they are doing project management as it ought to be done.

Most of us, however, are unlikely to have the opportunity. Nor are we likely to have the inclination. This mode of managing is a struggle against a world unwilling to understand our perspective. The political forces that drive the demand for project management are driving it in the opposite direction.

There are other options. We can share the mistrust of short-termism without being so obsessively inclusive, or quite so perfectionist in our ambitions. We can be socially aware, and bring in those off-stage voices when it suits us, but also find other ways to re-align our projects in useful directions without putting ourselves in the firing line all the time. To those considering an attempt at playing Master of Ceremonies I would say your first priority is to look after yourself. You cannot save the project management world. Good enough outcomes, for your projects and for yourself, are sufficient.

9. PLAYING THE RESHAPER

In control of the plot

For the Reshaper the world of projects is intensely political, inhabited by diverse groups of people, with different agenda, engaged in power struggles, each endeavouring to come out on top. Some players in this environment are sharp operators, and will succeed. Others will be found wanting, not up to scratch, and will fail.

Being a Reshaper is about understanding the 'realities' of this political world and acting to align the project with the agenda of the powers that will prevail. It is about knowing which way the wind is blowing and choosing a project journey that has the wind behind it.

Our previous archetypes have accepted a project plot that has been written for them by others. Even the Master of Ceremonies, committed to opening the project to the voices of diverse parties, has accepted the basic premises that determine what the project is essentially about. The outside parties, when invited to join in the project, are expected to contribute to a fixed conception of the project's basic aims.

Our Reshaper is inherently suspicious of such fixed ideas.

The norms of the Project Management profession do not encourage the Reshaper. It is for others to decide on the nature of a project, and for the Project Manager to deliver it. The Reshaper thinks this stance is foolhardy. It is not good sense to be caught out being the manager of an inherently poor project. If we find ourselves in such a situation it is better to correct it rather than struggle on against the odds. We do not want to persist with a losing game. Better to redefine that game, to change the rules.

Our project might be 'poor' in several respects. It could just be infeasible: badly designed, overambitious, lacking the right people to complete it, or fraught with indefinable uncertainties. However competent we are, we risk being labelled as the manager who failed, and as we have noted, many people find this difficult to take (even with the prospect of later redemption).

Some projects may be unreasonably difficult. If there are continuing tribal struggles these will sap the energy of the project, and our work as managers to press forward will be undermined by demoralising opposition, arguments and sideshows. It is far better to bind the project plot to a powerful agenda so it can go forward with confidence.

Furthermore, as a Reshaper I will take a personal interest in whatever that powerful agenda might be. Is it good for me and my ambitions? I am not a neutral observer, a hired servant with no stake in the outcome. My cherished career is being carried on the back of this project, and I have a duty to myself to be concerned about where it is taking me. I need to be a winner, and so I need to be in a winning team, playing a winning game.

Reshapers are thus a form of Expert, but not in the technologies involved in the project, nor in the intricacies of Project Management practice. Rather they are experts on projects as strategic artefacts in a political world. They understand how projects are used by powerful players to further their strategies. They understand how projects can be reshaped and redefined; how they can be re-directed to support different ends. And they understand how to make the most of projects for their own good.

To exemplify these principles I summarise four project stories here, which are quite diverse in terms of their domain, and also in the forms of intervention that might be available to our Reshapers.

James is manager of a business improvement project, re-engineering the operating processes of a property management company. In accordance with his agreement with the parent organisation, he has taken shares in the company, which they can buy back from him at an agreed date. He therefore has a huge personal stake in the project's success. The work progresses well at first, but then he realises that some of his co-managers, employed by the parent company, are deliberately slowing down the progress of the project. James realises that they hope to depress the share price at which they will buy his exit from the project. For them the 'plot' of the project is about discovering plans to improve business performance without actually implementing them. James responds to this with a radical strategy, finding financial backers who will enable him to engineer a hostile take-over bid for the company.

Robert has been engaged as an external project manager to bring in a new administration system for a pension scheme. However he soon discovers that the plans are overambitious, and there are Directors of the company who are more concerned about a financial agenda: the planned disposal of a large part of the company together with the transfer of the relevant pensions. Robert responds by forming an alliance with one of these Directors, cutting back the administration functionality to be provided by the project, and re-orientating its scope to support the financial agenda.

Kieran has been appointed to his first management position, implementing a major internet website. Although it starts well, he soon realises that his employer's financial position is far from healthy. He manoeuvres himself into a role where he can investigate the finances and discovers a major shortfall. His current job is vital to expanding his experience to support his career, so he continues in his role, while warning allies in the client and contractor organisations so they can protect themselves from exposure to the likely financial collapse. The original website project thus appears to be very dubious, but Kieran's new project 'plot', now about his own career, is on track.

Jonathan is manager of a government-funded university research project. The project is dependent on collecting data from industrial partners. A few months into the project these partners withdraw (for various reasons). This is an unlucky turn of fortune. However Jonathan and his colleagues revise the project scope, to use existing research material to create output (academic papers). The initial purpose of the project, to carry out original research, has now been discarded, but the project is completed successfully, so far as Jonathan and his team are concerned. The government funding agency is not concerned by the change in plot.

Can these types of shift be applied to any project? In each of these four cases it might be argued that the project has hit a sticky patch, and radical action, setting the project in a new direction, must be taken to get it out of that patch.

Without such an imperative to change, however, any project can still offer possibilities to a sharp operator. There will always be potential for re-realignment, to connect a project more soundly to that dominant agenda, to free it wherever possible from those energy-sapping tribal struggles. Our Reshaper will always be on the lookout, scanning the horizon for opportunities that can be taken to change course, especially if such a change offers enhancement to his or her own career.

This type of action, however, also carries hazards. If we align more strongly with one person's agenda, then someone else is being disenfranchised, their own view of the plot discarded. We may be making enemies on the way, and leaving grudges in our wake.

The Reshaper's performance

The first component of the Reshaper's performance concerns the wider social environment, the attention paid to understanding the tribal interests that surround the project. If these are not clear, then it will be necessary to find out what is going on.

James, carefully watching his co-managers, spots the new agenda emerging:

> *They were more focused on the fact that we had got a very good deal and were going to make a very large amount of money out of the transaction. And so in the six months to [...] we started to see that they were seeking to slow down our expansion to prevent us doing some of the strategic steps that we had agreed, and they did that because they could see that if they could learn from us what could be done, and get to the point of [...] when they had the right to buy us, they could buy us out for a relatively modest amount in relation to a much higher potential amount, and then in theory go on and do what we had told them, and make a lot more money for themselves.*

Robert, soon after his arrival as manager for the pensions office project, is concerned about the apparent lack of interest on the part of the company executive. He must first find out what they are thinking:

> *I decided to bridge the gap and get closer to the executive, and especially to Ken [the Chief Executive] and to his deputy Belinda, who was also the Director of Administration. I soon realized they didn't really have confidence in the project, or in the ability of [the technical people ...] to deliver it. Their only serious topic of conversation was an impending sale of a large part of [the parent company] and the need to pass on a big part of the pension fund with that sale. They talked only of the company's liabilities, and the need to divest these at the time of the sale.*

And Kieran discovers that something is seriously amiss:

> *As we were rounding out on this [phase] our senior web developer left, and out the door informed me that she hadn't*

> been paid in weeks. I myself was being paid irregularly.
>
> ... I began to dig into the financial picture. They were very secretive, but as a side project I helped them develop their presentations to the financiers, so I had understood at least what we were telling the financiers. I found a much more corrupt organization at the highest levels.

The Reshaper takes soundings from the surrounding world, gets an inkling, perhaps a mere smell, that something is not quite making sense, and moves to investigate. This can be just a matter of talking and listening, or, as for Kieran, manipulating arrangements to get at the information he needs.

The rhetoric that supports this questioning is the duality that contrasts sound well-founded projects with those that are unsound. Some projects forever teeter on the brink of being inviable and vulnerable to collapse; others feel sound and safe. Robert's discovery that the executive *"didn't really have confidence"* is replaced, after he has made his move, by a belief that *"Although the shift had been painful it now felt like the right project, and we moved on."* This argument, in some form, sits behind every shift in the plot.

Since the purpose of a change in course concerns alignment with other people's agenda, the move is always founded in some form of alliance. Robert aligns his project with an agenda of big finance and divestment, and to do so he must connect with those for whom that agenda is primary:

> I formed an alliance with Belinda, and together we brought this big finance agenda to the foreground ... Belinda and I took control and refocused the project on supporting the divestment. We visited the supplier together, where we struck out swathes of the project scope, optimizing the new system to deal with the financial transactions.

Kieran, in deciding to switch his allegiance away from his current corrupt employer, declares common cause with those others, the honest players in the industry with whom his future rests:

> I decided that I had to protect future contractors and vendors, without getting into any legal entanglements myself.

> *I quietly told our vendors and contractors what the situation was, and they backed out.*

It is these alliances that provide us with the levers that can be used to force that change of direction. Robert has Belinda's executive power at his side as he changes the project scope. James brings big financial backing to his planned move to make a bid for the parent company:

> *We explored that with our investors, we needed to raise about [£ millions] or thereabouts sterling, in order to make it a viable strategy ... So we moved into a period of three months where we were negotiating with investment houses, private equity houses, etc, and it was a compelling proposition and over the subsequent three months in [...] we got three fully-backed offers that allowed us to present a formal take-over bid to the other party.*

So with allies and preparation, action can be taken, and opposition overcome.

Some deploy an open strategy to make their moves, with cards on the table. In preparing his game for the hostile takeover bid, James shows his hand to his opponent:

> *In going through that process I had a very good relationship with the Chief Executive on the other side and therefore I spent a lot of time talking to him, getting close to him, making sure this wasn't a surprise.*

Later, when the relationship gets less friendly, James has gained the high moral ground having kept the other party informed, and can claim his own good faith and honesty in comparison with the other party's duplicity.

Clearly Kieran, who is sabotaging his (albeit corrupt) employer's web development project, cannot take the same line, and must protect himself and his allies by keeping his hand closed. Similarly Jonathan, who is preserving his university research project by diverting its purpose from that agreed with its funders, will not publicise his new strategy. His funders in this case may not be particularly concerned, but they will not wish to draw attention to the fact that tax-payers' money is not being used as authorised.

I have been using a gaming metaphor because strategies are akin to those of a serious game player. This should not be taken as implying that the Reshaper is engaged in a random game of chance, gambling with the future. On the contrary, the moves are highly calculated, and arise from careful investigation and analysis. James is familiar with the details of his contracts, and his legal position. Kieran finds out the details of the project and company finances. These people are playing strategies for which they have done the calculations; they know they are going to win.

In summary, the Reshaper's performance lies in the re-invention of the project within its social context. Reshapers differ from other archetypes in their willingness to wade into the political mire and take radical action to divert the project, and with it their own position, to what they consider to be a more favourable direction. For other managers, change is an unfortunate imposition, which must be controlled. For the Reshaper change is an implement of identity creation. It is through discovering potential project changes, and making them happen, that a manager becomes a Reshaper.

In the world of winners and losers

As Reshapers our primary aim is to be there playing our part with those emerging as winners as the inter-tribal struggles play themselves out. We must avoid being cast with those other people, the losers, those who have failed to recognise the powerful agenda that is carrying the day.

When Kieran makes his decision to *"protect future contractors and vendors"* he is making his assessment about who will come out of this dangerous situation in credit. He decides that these people, the legitimate development industry, are his preferred future. He has concluded that his employers, the people who engaged him on this project, are no longer a winning option.

These switches of allegiance are part of the archetypal act. To perform it we need to cultivate a position of detachment. We will make a show of committing to a faction, but within us we know we may need to switch again. This detachment can give the illusion that we are merely playing games, as though we have found our way into a sporting team, and we are throwing ourselves into it for the thrill of being winners. But generally Reshapers are not engaged in anything as casual as this. They are driven by a real fear of losing, and need to save themselves by outplaying those who might degrade their positions, who might damage their identities as successful operators. The urge is to be in control of one's own future, or perhaps more pertinently to avoid the opposite, the horrifying prospect of finding oneself at the mercy of others. James's description of his point of decision, his moment of fluidity, is informative:

> *... and we decided that if we could, instead of being at the whim of the other party, who had the right to buy us out, if we took a major step, and stepped into the fight, and bought their whole group, then we would take over their top company, and effectively we would then own the whole lot ...*

We can read this moment as being a statement of crude financial ambition: that James's intent is to get rich quickly. However my own belief is that the heart of the matter lies in those words *"the whim of the other party"*. His most awful fear is that his future, for richer or for poorer, is to be decided by someone else. What is more, that someone else is driven by *"whims"* rather than by expert understanding. That is what drives him to his dramatic choice of strategy.

Through moves such as James's above, Reshapers can gain a sense of personal freedom. While other project managers are perpetually at the beck and call of political masters, Reshapers believe that their actions enable them to escape from this tyranny; they create the illusion (or self-delusion) that they are in control of their own destinies.

The flexibility of Reshapers, seen in their inclination to liberate themselves from their obligations to others, has an amoral aura. There is no loyalty. Today's alliance is fragile. Tomorrow we may see another advantageous change of tack and reshape our project, and our allegiances, yet again.

The lack of loyalty is not malicious. We have all met, in our organisational travels, that other beast, the Jungle Fighter, for whom all allies are potentially unreliable or treacherous, and all enemies must be crushed. This is not the attitude of the Reshaper. We do not think badly of those who have lost out to our moves; they are not dangerous enemies. They are good people, and have been good allies, but we have moved on, and they now have the misfortune to be in the wrong camp. James is at pains to point out:

> ... *and actually the Chief Exec of that business and I have remained professional friends despite the stand-off that we got to*

However our lack of commitment, with its apparent amorality, is potentially dangerous. We do not want to be seen as completely lacking in integrity, or as not having any sense of value. To mitigate this we have a powerful rhetoric we can use to justify ourselves, the framing narrative of the 'tough world'. In the rough and tumble of the competitive business world people lose out and get displaced. That's how it is. If they backed the wrong horse they will lose. We can claim a sort of project Darwinism: the survival of the fittest. Those who are sharp, alert and knowing deserve to survive; and those who are not deserve to go under.

As James leaves his crucial meeting with his opponents, he notes:

> *And we left that ... meeting very promptly having been very professional and very proper about it. And we did everything within the corporate capacity that we had, but we were, you know, just sharper than them, in frank terms.*

In James' eyes this explanation, of just being sharper, makes it inevitable that he and his associates will come out on top.

Robert uses a similar rhetoric to explain his actions. He recognises his disloyalty to the original project owner:

> *She had brought me into the project, but now I had betrayed her, conspiring with Belinda to undermine her and decimate her plans. She left the company soon afterwards.*

But it is a hard world, and good reasons can be found for taking a course that advances one's own position while betraying loyalties to others:

Firstly, by pushing through a dodgy project I would have done myself no favours with the project management community ... Secondly, and crucially, the vultures – Belinda and her friends on the executive – were already circling overhead. As soon as they smelt failure they would have pounced. There was never a benign option – a route we could follow where everyone got what they wanted, and where nobody got hurt. So in the end I'm sure it was right to go with the most powerful agenda and realign the project to support the big finance manoeuvres. It was always going to happen, so it was best to get on with it.

In these situations the play of appearing to be open can be helpful. If a decision is to be claimed as inevitable, then it is better if I can, like Robert, make the switch of strategy appear as a necessary collective decision, made in the reality of a heartless competitive world. It is better that the tough world should be blamed for a tough decision, than it should appear to be a manifestation of my own self-interested deviousness, cunning, deception or trickery.

Playing and moving on

Reshapers have a big impact. They get reputations for being effective managers, people who can take action and make things happen. The ability to shape their world is considered, by business leaders, to be a valuable attribute. Reshapers are in demand, with good reason. If, as they claim, they are making better projects, then that must lead to better, more socially beneficial outcomes. However, as we have noted, they often also leave damage in their wake.

Since Reshapers are, behind this social face, primarily playing for themselves, they play the role with some intensity, with dramatic actions supported by carefully crafted stories of justification. It is a demanding style of management for its players, who must forever attend to the politics around the project, sense what is going on, and make direction-changing decisions.

For those of you who wish to play this archetype, the entry gate may at first sight appear straightforward. For example, as an

Analyst or an Enforcer finding yourself in that sticky patch you can in principle widen your brief and look for a structural move, one that will reframe the project as a way to free it from its troubles. With good fortune you may find such an option. However established Reshapers will be several steps ahead of you. They will already have looked at the politics of the situation, well before the sticky patch was reached. Their sense of personal crisis, their fear of being underdogs, has already driven them into action, to investigate, analyse, plan and scheme. The new project crisis, that sticky patch, appears to them as the opportunity they have been waiting for, which enables them to implement a reshaping plan that was already in their minds. Becoming a Reshaper is not so much a one-off attempt to reshape today's project, but more a matter of entering their world of politics and manoeuvres.

The Reshaper's life as a project manager can feel rather aimless: project plots devised and revised, with little commitment to any particular project destination. What's it all about?

Those early in their careers, or newly playing this archetype, have an answer to this question. Their first destination is to establish their own managerial reputation. Kieran, for example is being an apprentice. He has immersed in his chosen field of website development and has at the same time picked up the Reshaper's skills of political understanding and action. His employer's project, in our example, gets nowhere, but his career future has been greatly enhanced by his experience.

For those of us later on in life and career the purpose of being a manager in this mode is less clear. We play our part in one situation, and then another, and perhaps another. It is as though we must demonstrate to ourselves that this is what we do; but we have no higher purpose. Before many years have passed, we Reshapers can lose interest in project management as a profession (if we have not already been upended by a sharper operator). When this happens that desire to escape, to free ourselves from the whims of those less able decision-makers, will drive us to move onwards, to new fields, new careers.

We need a new stage for a new performance. Our time for playing project manager has come to an end.

10. PROJECT LIVES: ARCHETYPES AND CAREERS

In the previous six chapters I have presented six archetypes: six distinct ways in which the role of project manager can be performed. Each is self sufficient, a way of being a project manager. If one of these archetypes suits your personal inclination, and you have found a place where you can play it, then that is enough.

However my purpose in this final chapter is to move on beyond that single-mode view, and consider matters concerning multi-archetype players: those who acquire the abilities, and find the opportunities, to perform in more than one mode.

There are two lines of thinking to consider. The first concerns the individual who has the capacity to put on a coherent performance of any of several archetypes, perhaps within the course of a single project. The second concerns the matter of personal development: the potential to progress from one archetype to another during the course of a career in project management.

The perfect project manager?

Considering the project super-manager, could there be a person who can play all archetypes?

We could interpret this question in terms of language and

communication. We might make an analogy with the Holy Roman Emperor Charles V, who is reputed to have spoken in Spanish to God, in Italian to women, in French to men, and in German to his horse. Is there an equivalent project manager? Such a manager might speak: as an Analyst in the project team, as an Enforcer to financial backers and to recalcitrant contractors, as an Expert to critics, as an Impresario to customers, as a Master of Ceremonies to the wider public, and as a Reshaper to allies and fellow plotters.

Considered purely as a matter of appropriate language, this is an informative exercise. Any manager will find it useful to understand these skills. It is good to know how to speak to people in a way that addresses their concerns. Our Master of Ceremonies, injecting reflective pauses into the project to hear the voices of excluded outside parties, must at the same time find words to speak to financial backers, to assure them that their money is not being squandered. "Regardless of this pause", he or she will say, "the project is under tight control." Likewise, a rigid Enforcer, who has just quashed a new and creative initiative in the name of meeting the programme, must be able to speak to customers, and assure them that everything possible is being done to deliver a product that is admirably suited to their purposes. It is important to know what people want to hear, and to address their expectations.

But speaking is not all. Your words in Italian may be well received by women, but they do not make you into an Italian. Our concern is with crisis moments in projects, when we must propose a way forward, presenting ourselves as the person with the authority to point the way. To do that we must act and speak in character, modelled on a single archetype, and possessing a specific proposal for moving on. We can slant our explanations to suit different audiences, but our overall story must be coherent. We cannot point in many directions at the same time, and expect people to follow.

A stronger interpretation of the super-manager question concerns situation. Can we postulate a person who adopts and plays the part of an archetype selected as appropriate to the situation of the day? Is this the perfect project manager? Might I aspire to be such a person, one who possesses the wherewithal, the authority, the costume, the stage, the language for each archetype, and each day puts on the act appropriate to the project situation at hand?

My response to this question is to object to it. I object on two counts.

Firstly I want to ask who is in control of defining the situation. A difficult project situation does not present itself fully formed, incontestable, like a leaking pipe to be replaced by the plumber. Project problems are social and complex. To be skilful project managers we must first take action to define the nature of a problem. In pursuing that definition we have latitude, and will interpret a situation to suit ourselves and our ambitions. If it suits my agenda to be an Enforcer, I will interpret any situation as chaotic, needing control through my enforcing actions, even when others think we could usefully allow some flexibility. Alternatively when others might complain that the project is out of control, I don't have to agree. As a Reshaper, for example, I might welcome that moment, with its atmosphere of chaotic indecision, because I can turn it into an opportunity to reshape the project and propel it in a new direction. There is no objective concrete situation that determines the person I must be to deal with it.

So there is no multiplicity of situation types that demands a similar multiplicity in the archetypes I can play. I have choice. I can be a good enough manager playing a very limited repertoire.

My second objection to the concept of the perfect project manager concerns its purpose. Who is asking for such a person? Who profits from postulating this ideal project manager?

The custodians of the profession, of course, will gain. They can set themselves up as arbiters to enhance their own agenda of running the profession. They could define criteria for assessing performances, and have managers take tests and undergo assessments to tick off their achievement level for each archetype. It will not matter that you may be playing five archetypes. To claim your black belt qualification you will need to pass the exam for the sixth. Colleges and other training establishments will be able sell comprehensive accredited courses. If they have their way you will surely feel guilt; embarrassed that you are missing one or another persona on your tick-list of archetype qualifications.

But how does it profit a project manager to be such a person? To be a project manager it is sufficient to perform one archetype. We may well have invested substantial effort in developing a public performance, establishing ourselves as a credible and authentic player of that archetype. To suggest that we might now play another introduces an additional burden, another criterion of worthiness we managers must suffer. It is another opportunity for us to be measured and found wanting. It is another pressure, and an unnecessary one.

There is no imperative, demanding that we strive to be that supposedly perfect project manager who encompasses all archetypes.

Despite my objections, some managers may well wish to adopt a multi-archetype persona, and may perhaps gain personal satisfaction from the virtuosity, the variety and breadth, of their managerial performances. However I believe that to go in this direction it is far better to expand our repertoire only when a good opportunity presents itself, and only if that new option suits our personal inclinations and ambitions.

My own preference is to consider the multi-archetype possibilities in terms of a career journey, in which we occasionally choose to move forwards from one style to another.

The project manager's career

I have no prescription here for career paths. There is no norm, nor any linear progression through archetype performances that leads onwards and upwards to some higher status or goal.

We should be wary of any notion of a career plan. The paths people follow in what they later describe, with hindsight, as their careers, are rarely routes they have chosen in advance or planned. In reality my 'career' is a step-by-step progression. It is a matter of opportunities: of spotting a chance, recognising it as a good direction in which I might go, and finding a way to take it. Carpe diem!

However there are some natural progressions. Some modes of managing, supplemented by experience, lead naturally onwards to others. There are well-worn paths of learning and advancing that can make sound sense. The notion of a journey along a path will not preclude flexibility, the option to return to an earlier style of working, revisiting the scene of an old archetype and trying it out again.

My plan here is to inspect these career paths. Firstly we will briefly re-look at each archetype, noting its gates of entry and exit. We will then address some general principles of direction: the drivers that motivate individuals to choose to seek opportunities that can lead them in one particular direction or another.

Analyst

The Analyst is an entry-level archetype. Thinking self-propelled workers can, without too much difficulty, expand their scope to lead others in similar work. They can learn the basic formal skills of project management, acquire the 'Project Manager' title, and gradually take on the added responsibilities. These are clever people, living an existence of solving problems, and resolving glitches. To become managers they learn to do this on behalf of others.

Sally's two stories, which we looked at earlier, took place six years apart, and show a path people might well take into and through the Analyst mode.

In her first story she was a new manager, threatened by the hostility of a senior manager. We see her as an enthusiastic and committed individual, but someone who was slow to notice the plot being hatched around her, and who then underwent a cycle of depression followed, eventually, by renewal.

In her later story, she sensed a political storm on the horizon, and acted early to pre-empt it. We see a confident and politically aware person, who presents her analysis of the situation to senior managers and persuades them to act. Her six years as a manager have brought maturity in her style, and a wider social awareness.

The second story also, with its interest in the political resolutions to the perceived problem, also carries her in the direction of becoming a Reshaper. It is not a big step from here to get more political in her manoeuvres.

Will other archetypes choose to play the Analyst? Will those who have moved on retain the Analyst archetype in their repertoire? In its favour it is a useful ability. There will always be occasions when some thorough analysis, delving into complexities, can show you a route forward. Furthermore, the close involvement with the team, producing good things, can be very satisfying.

On the other hand it is hard work. Those who perform another mode have tasted a more sophisticated form of power; they have found the ability to control others without having to go through the effort of understanding what those others actually do. So it is unlikely that managers who have moved on will be inclined to return to playing Analyst. If analysis is needed, it is usually preferable to get someone else to do it for you.

However there will be some people, in particular Reshapers, who cannot trust others to analyse on their behalf, and will sometimes find the need to immerse themselves in details in order to plot their next move.

Enforcer

The Enforcer, too, is an entry-level archetype. We have seen Enforcers in action as powerful established players, with authority, but we have also seen the role performed very effectively by young upstarts. For such people this archetype offers a rapid rise up the managerial tree, and is clearly very attractive. Many of them, perhaps seeing no need to develop any alternative style, adopt this as their permanent single way of managing. They are always in demand, get their promotions, and keep doing it. Being an Enforcer can be a career in itself. It may lead to tumbles when things go wrong, but competent players can rise again.

Those who play other archetypes can usefully have an Enforcer within them. It is a good idea to rehearse the skills. You can sometimes save trouble and avoid hard work by demanding that others fulfil their responsibilities. For example we saw that Frankie, entering her rule-bending Impresario mode, needed to establish some stability in her surroundings, and laid down the law to her suppliers. You cannot break the rules on all fronts at the same time, she observed.

However such action, pragmatically dipping into the mode, doing a bit of enforcing, is essentially a sideshow to your main managerial performance, whatever form that takes. It is not the same as the massive performance – the full-blown managerial stance, acting as the agent of order and control – put on by those who have chosen to invest their careers in being Enforcers.

Expert

People who become Expert project managers arrive in the role from being discipline experts. Becoming a project manager is a way of reinforcing their expert status, taking responsibility for imposing their expert knowledge across the project. There is no entry through the gate to this archetype without the passport of expertise.

Experts, in general, stay within the role. The sense of worth the position gives them is not to be thrown away lightly.

Despite these elements of permanence, there are some who come in temporarily. Some take it up as a career starter. There are technical industries where managers are expected to have some gravitas. There are the places where nobody is allowed to be a manager before they have at least ten years experience. It is a long managerial apprenticeship, and there is an advantage to be gained by adding a project management qualification on the way. Such people may later drop their Expert status (and their project management role too) when they find an opportunity to move on to higher positions.

Reshapers too may sometimes poke their heads into the Expert zone to safeguard their position. A situation may arise when they fear finding themselves at the whim of experts. We can note the intensity with which James immersed himself in learning the practices and procedures of the property management business to gain an advantage over those he wished to outmanoeuvre.

Impresario

There are some privileged to work in the arts or charities who are given a free hand, for whom Impresario is the norm for managing projects. They are unlikely to venture into other modes, nor into jobs in more constrained industries.

For those employed in these more constrained organisations, whether corporate or public, the Impresario is a possible breakout route from other archetypes, such as Enforcer or Analyst. People who make this move need the motivation (belief in the value of what they do), supporters, and awareness of the social and political implications of their intended rule-bending.

Once they have played the part, having gained their sense of freedom, practitioners are likely to retain the Impresario in their repertoire, and will revert to it in their hour of need.

Master of Ceremonies

The Master of Ceremonies is a mature position. Its players need authority and the trust of senior managers, and are socially responsible. They arrive in the role from previous positions of responsibility. Masters of Ceremonies think their way of being a manager is inherently right, so are unlikely to move on.

Those performing other archetypes may wish to try out this role, but it takes time to develop the social standing the role demands, and it cannot be taken on lightly.

Reshaper

The Reshaper's performance requires management experience. Some progress there from having been Analysts, having extended their analytical scope beyond the technical to include social and political matters. People are driven to this mode by their fear of failure, and dislike of being at the whim of others. The role needs awareness of organisation and politics, and so people taking it up it will already be caught up in organisational affairs.

Reshaper project managers tend to take on a few contests, and then move on, looking for new fields of opportunity, probably leaving the project management profession.

Towards competence

While we cannot define anything as clear as a standard career path, we can however see some general directions. There are drivers, reasons why people prefer to perform one archetype, or move on to another. These drivers can underlie those longer personal stories that people can relate about their careers and lives. They are also often evident in the shorter day-to-day stories told by project managers.

The first career driver I note concerns competence. The primary inclination of our players is to develop confidence and fluency within a chosen archetype. They find an archetype that is personally appealing to them, and try to achieve some form of excellence, of virtuosity within that mode of performance. For many people, being good at their job, in whatever particular style they have chosen to play it, brings a sense of security, and so appears to be more important than finding a new way of operating.

But nonetheless many of us do move on, adding breadth to our competence. We gain social, legal, political knowledge and becoming more adept at managing our social environment. Management life is full of difficulties and upsets, and we continually learn how we can better handle them. We find more levers, ways of making our lives easier, ways of standing back and looking around rather than immersing in work.

In particular this extended knowledge takes us onwards from the Analyst mode. We learn how we could become Impresario, Master of Ceremonies or Reshaper. On this basis I consider these three to be more advanced archetypes. They require a greater social and political understanding than the entry-level archetypes of Analyst and Enforcer, or the science-driven Expert.

Towards personal autonomy

Another important influence on the direction of individual travel concerns personal autonomy. Organisations can be considered as arenas in which power relationships are played out. For individual managers, their attitude and response to power can motivate them towards a desire to perform in particular modes in preference to others.

Analysts and Enforcers are thoroughly embedded in the normal hierarchical power relationships that pervade organisations. They are party to an implicit understanding of mutual support. They act as servants to their senior management masters, who in return look after their well-being as trusted servants. Senior managers have good reason to place their trust here. Remote from actual work, they live in a state of fear about what is happening, or not happening, at the sharp end of whatever their business may be: "Is anybody doing anything? Can I trust them to get it right?" Analysts and Enforcers respond to these fears, proving reassurances. The Analysts, in big-brother fashion, find out exactly what is going on and explain it to their senior managers, who can then act with confidence. The Enforcers, by extracting commitments from unreliable contributors and enforcing compliance, provide assurance that all is in order.

Many people are content to work in this way; they get satisfaction from being useful to important people. Others are not so content. For them hierarchical power is oppressive, and they look for ways to escape its domination.

The Expert archetype offers a professional autonomy. Like independent craftsmen offering specialised services, Experts seek to set themselves up as free agents, their own masters. Their allegiance is to their trade, and they think of their relationships with the lords of the workplace as being founded on agreements between equals.

Impresarios establish their zone of independence – their personal fiefdom. This may be an entire project where they have negotiated an unfettered freedom of action with their patrons. It may alternatively be a zone of defiance or insubordination: a secret project, or a rule-bending excursion. By creating this personal territory they assert their independence, under the eyes of the corporate controllers.

The Master of Ceremonies seeks to defuse the simple bipolar power structure, placing himself or herself, together with owners, sponsors and everyone, within a wider social context, distributing power to diverse interests. "I am not your servant, I am the servant of everyone", is the assertion through which

Masters of Ceremonies attempt to negate imposed power.

Reshapers deny the master-servant relationship. From their perspective all players in the territory of the project are political actors, pulling whatever levers they can find to achieve their ends. As a Reshaper project manager I believe I have as much right as anyone to mould strategies and events. My bosses may have an employment or contractual lever, but I have other levers – inside knowledge, outside allies, strategic moves – that I can bring to bear. By creating illusions of autonomy and freedom, Reshapers mentally liberate themselves from unjust rule.

We see above three basic orientations to games of power. The first is to accept the role of servant. The second is to find alternative sources of power, and use these to resist. The third is to join in, and become a player of the game.

These issues of power and autonomy affect people differently, and do not necessarily drive a specific career progression through archetypes. However those who have entered the profession through a door fortuitously open to them, such as Analyst or Enforcer, will look for a way to move on if they are not comfortable with their subservient position in relation to power. Similarly, people who have achieved a role that provides greater autonomy are unlikely to throw that away and accept a return to a more submissive relationship. The career trend we see is thus generally towards increasing autonomy.

Playing the project manager: in conclusion

And so we conclude our journey of understanding on the subject of project managers and their performance.

I have outlined the principles of project manager identities, and how they are performed. I have presented six distinct archetypes that exemplify the modes of performance that are available to players on the project management stage.

By adopting a person-centred approach to the subject we have revealed, through the stories of individual managers, the personal benefits that people can gain from their engagement in the project management profession. Why do people pursue this occupation?

The answer to this question is not merely economic. It is

evident that people find much personal satisfaction in being project managers. That sense of their own value, as we have witnessed, is very varied. We have seen a plain and simple satisfaction in personal advancement. We have also seen gratification gained from the experience of close working with colleagues, from a being useful contributor to corporate and public endeavours, from contributing to something worthwhile, from supporting social inclusion, and from being appreciated for this contribution. These and other rewards encourage and sustain those working in this field, and their belief that their chosen career is worthwhile. The occupation of project management provides diverse opportunities, to people with diverse interests.

If you are a project manager, the existence of different ways of performing the role, exemplified in the archetypes, provides options, a degree of choice, for you to change your way of being a manager to better match your personal preferences and ambitions. If you choose to take a new direction there will be obstacles put in your way. There will be others, pursuing their own agenda, who will resist. They may use tactics both fair and foul, perhaps making personal attacks, and denying your right to play the role in the manner you choose. As evidence against you they may cite all manner of personal objections: to your gender, your race, your age, or merely the look in your eye. However the evidence shows that if you have the right basic resources for an archetype – the support of allies, the skills, the knowledge – then you can play it.

To do so you must find your opportunity. We have seen that this is likely to come at a time of uncertainty. At such a time, new thinking, from a new you, can become a credible route out of that uncertainty. The link to the broader story of your organisation is also crucial. You must find a resonance between the narrative that frames your chosen archetype and issues that are current. Some of these framing narratives – the problem and solution of the Analyst, or the drive to control of the Enforcer – are usually easily connected to current concerns. The relevance of other archetypal performances may need to be developed using your rhetorical skills.

For those entering the profession and trying to emerge as decision makers, or for those in the profession who realise they would rather be a different sort of decision maker, opportunities for development and change can be found. It is my hope that the matters I have set out – the principles of identity development, the details of resources and skills, and of coherent and effective archetypal performances – will provide readers with guidance they can use to set out in new directions, pursuing reputation and career. Above all, I hope that the perspective I have adopted, of giving precedence to the reality of the person in preference to the project, will provide encouragement. Your working life is the stage for the performance of your personal ambitions, and these are your priority when you play the project manager.

APPENDIX: NOTES ON RESEARCH AND LITERATURE

This appendix presents an outline of my research into the performance of project managers, and the literature that has influenced my work, from the disciplines of project management, organisation studies and psychology. It is a summary which is not comprehensive in any academic sense. I have made no systematic search of relevant literature. It more reflects a journey of learning, from one idea to something linked and onwards, prompted by reading, discussions and reactions to my published papers.

Topics presented here are broadly in the order in which they arise in chapters 1 to 3.

Chapter 1 – Project Managers as Performers

My central concepts, the interconnection between identity and social sense, and how a performance can be used to take control of a situation, are founded on the work of Erving Goffman, and his *Performance of Self in Everyday Life* (1959), which provides pragmatic guidance on what constitutes an effective social performance.

In a work context, Karl Weick, in *Sensemaking in Organizations* (1995), takes a similar perspective. Sensemaking, he tells us, is founded on identity.

Sixteen stories have been provided to me, for my research, by real-life managers. These stories provide the basis for what I have written concerning the principles of project manager performances and the archetypes. Within each archetype chapter I have also drawn from other stories to exemplify how the archetype is played. These arise from my own experience and research, previously presented in *Making Sense of Project Realities* (Smith, 2007).

The methodology I have used to analyse and interpret stories is described in detail in a published paper (Smith, 2011). The analysis of the stories follows a systematic inspection of the texts of the stories, based on techniques presented by Boje (2001). His methods provide a means of extracting rich understandings of the thinking that underlies the texts: the rhetorical performance, the implicit assumptions, the silencing of alternative stories, and other matters.

My style of research, the interrogation of the actual lives of project practitioners, is in line with the preferred approach of the discipline of Critical Management Studies. The need for such research is argued by Cicmil (2006). A review of the project management discipline from this perspective can be found in *Making Projects Critical* (Hodgson and Cicmil, 2006). Within that book, the notion of the project management profession as a personal prison is discussed by Lindgren and Packendorff (2006).

My interest in the performance of individuals also addresses matters raised by Schön (1983), who emphasises the importance of understanding a profession in terms of what its practitioners actually do, as opposed to what its institutions claim they do.

Chapter 2 – Being a Project Manager

My research question ("Tell me about a project challenge and how you handled it") generates a decided bias towards those who have decided to act managerially. This is a deliberate policy, because decision-making managers are my primary interest. My findings display a marked contrast with other research into the lives of project managers. Research through interviews, reported by Paton et al (2010), reveals that many so-called Project Managers do very little in the way of decision-making.

The emergence of individuals as managers, in some form, is central to the study of identity construction in the workplace. A personal reflexive case-study, on the experience of becoming 'manager', has been written by Parker (2004).

The form of resilience that is central to my discussion, the ability to change and re-invent oneself at a time of adversity, is a tenet of Personal Construct Psychology (Kelly, 1955), and particularly Kelly's basic assumption of 'constructive alternativism', ie that our "interpretations of the universe are subject to revision or replacement".

A very thorough survey of the alternatives that people find

for understanding life's meanings appears in *Meanings of Life* (Baumeister, 1991). This work includes a discussion of the career option as a source of life's meaning, and makes observations on its limitations and drawbacks.

The multiplicity of our identities, the diverse versions of self that we enact in our personal and working lives, is the subject of *The Saturated Self* (Gergen,1991).

My comments on fluidity and choice are again related to the thinking of Kelly, and to alternativism.

Concerning typologies, there are many that address personality, these being well summarised by Totton and Jacobs (2001). My primary interest however is with typologies of social performances, or archetypes. I have chosen to found these on matters of authority – the identity of those having the power to speak. The essence of this issue – of speaking and having authority – is discussed by Foucault (1972).

The most relevant comparison I have found for my proposed archetypes is with those defined by Maccoby (1977) in *The Gamesman*, but even this is problematic. Maccoby actually treats social performances as being ingrained individual characteristics (based on Freudian psychodynamic personality types). His management type descriptions define the essence of who they are as people. For each type, he describes their manner of being managers, but then goes on to describe their whole lives: their hobbies, their politics, and the sorts of wives (sic) they have. For my archetypes, I limit my observations to their style of being managers, extending my view only on matters of the logic of where the role and its style of managing may lead.

Despite my objection to his position, there are actually close parallels between my archetypes and those of Maccoby, briefly:
- My Analyst and Enforcer can be considered variants of his Company Man
- My Expert is similar to his Craftsman (including the characteristic career longevity)
- My Reshaper is similar, in orientation and tactics, to his Gamesman (although I do not agree with his game-playing view of the role)

On the other hand, Maccoby also covers the Jungle Fighter, omitted from my discussion. Also, my more socially orientated types, the Impresario and Master of Ceremonies, appear to have no equivalent in Maccoby's analysis.

Another difference between my work and that of Maccoby concerns moral stance. He is pursuing a patriotic mission. US Corporations, he tells us, need more Gamesmen, fewer Jungle Fighters. For my part, I share his admiration for the Reshaper and Gamesman, but regard this liking as a matter of personal empathy on my part. Perhaps I wish I had played the role better myself. Overall however I have striven to sustain a stance of moral relativism: people should make their own choices about what is important to them, and put on performances that enact those choices. I have no messages for nations or corporations.

Chapter 3 − Getting Hold of the Plot

The concept of identity as founded on resources, but emerging from performance, is presented by Linstead and Linstead (2005).

Behind my discussion of individual stories and framing narratives there are several important theoretical issues, for example:
- the connection between the story as told now, to the researcher, and the narratives that informed actions at the time of the events;
- the story told now as a part of a longer story about the individual's life and developing identity;
- the story told by an individual as a manifestation of a wider communal story.

These issues are covered in depth by Carr (1986) in *Time History and Narrative*, and in terms of narrative identity (based on the philosophy of Paul Ricoeur), by Mallett and Wapshott (2011).

Some of the manager stories (although not all) display the importance of a practice community, in the manner described by Wenger (1998) in his *Communities of Practice*.

The narratives actually deployed by storytellers (revealed in chapters 4 to 9) cover a wide spectrum, going well beyond the traditional conception of project management as an administrative and control function. This was to be expected in the light of the directions of thinking proposed by the Rethinking

APPENDIX: NOTES ON RESEARCH AND LITERATURE

Project Management Network, as reported by Winter et al (2006), and in my own book, Smith (2007). A survey of the multiplicity of perspectives for thinking about projects and their management can be found in *Images of Projects* by Winter and Szczepanek (2009). Projects and their performance are presented as subjects of social science by Flyvbjerg (2001).

There is a view, based on the work of Foucault noted earlier, that personal psychology is not relevant to the investigation of managerial practice. Authority is embedded in the managerial role, and the manner of its practice defines who you are. However my concern is to support the individual, and for this endeavour matters of personal wherewithal – what a person is or is not able to do – are highly important, affecting the decisions individuals make concerning how they will play a managerial part: the sort of manager they might choose to try to become.

On the topic of the need to possess a social repertoire, which I have discussed only briefly, Goffman (1959) has much advice.

My discussion of management rhetoric draws firstly on Boje (2001). I have taken the term 'duality' from his analytical techniques. Boje's purpose is one of deconstruction. He provides techniques we can use to understand how individuals use language to wield power. For him, analysis of text is a subversive activity. Through analysis we can find out how a particular version of the 'plot' has been privileged, and who has been silenced, and how. With this knowledge we can act to undermine the story as told, and hence shift the balance of power.

I have also drawn on *Beyond the Hype*, by Eccles and Nohria (1992). These authors too are interested in rhetoric, but as a positive and essential skill of managers. Their interest is in advising industry leaders on how to speak in a powerful manner.

Both books provide valuable advice, which can be used by the reader either to construct rhetoric, or to de-construct it, according to their own preference of the moment.

Further discussion of the hard work involved in creating coherent stories and presenting an identity can be found in Linstead and Linstead (2005), Ezzy (2005), and Mallett and Wapshott (2011).

BIBLIOGRAPHY

Baumeister, R. F. (1991), *Meanings of Life*, The Guilford Press

Boje, D. M. (2001), *Narrative Methods for Organizational & Communication Research*, Sage

Carr, D. (1986), *Time, Narrative and History*, Indiana University Press

Cicmil, S. (2006), 'Understanding project management practice through interpretive and critical research perspectives', *Project Management Journal* 37(2)

Eccles, R. G. and Nohria, N. (1992), *Beyond the Hype: Rediscovering the Essence of Management*, Harvard Business School Press

Ezzy, D. (2005), 'Theorizing narrative identity: symbolic interactionism and hermeneutics', in Linstead, A. and Linstead, S. (eds), *Organization and Identity,* Routledge

Flyvbjerg, B. (2001), *Making Social Science Matter*, Cambridge University Press

Foucault, M. (1972), *The Archaeology of Knowledge*, Tavistock

Gergen, K. J. (1991), *The Saturated Self,* Basic Books

Goffman, E. (1959), *The Presentation of Self in Everyday Life*, Pelican Books

Hodgson, D. and Cicmil, S. (2006), *Making Projects Critical*, Palgrave

Kelly, G. A. (1955), *The Psychology of Personal Constructs*, Norton

Lindgren, M. and Packendorff, J. (2006), 'Projects and prisons', in Hodgson, D. and Cicmil, S. (eds), *Making Projects Critical*, Palgrave

Linstead, A. and Linstead, S. (2005), *Organization and Identity,* Routledge

Maccoby, M. (1977), *The Gamesman: The New Corporate Leaders*, Secker & Warburg

Mallett, O. and Wapshott, R. (2011), 'The challenges of identity work: Developing Ricoeurian narrative identity in organisations', *Ephemera* 11(3)

Paton, S., Hodgson, D. and Cicmil, S. (2010), 'Who am I and what am I doing here? Becoming and being a project manager', *Journal of Management Development* 29 (2)

Parker, M. (2004), 'Becoming Manager: or, The Werewolf Looks Anxiously in the Mirror, Checking for Unusual Facial Hair', *Management Learning* 35 (1)

Schön, D. A. (1983), *The Reflective Practitioner*, Basic Books

Smith, C. (2007), *Making Sense of Project Realities: Theory, Practice and the Pursuit of Performance*, Gower

Smith, C. (2011), 'Understanding project manager identities: a framework for research', *International Journal of Managing Projects in Business* 4 (4)

Totton, N. and Jacobs, M. (2001), *Character and Personality Types*, Open University Press

Weick, K. E. (1995), *Sensemaking in Organizations*, Sage

Wenger, E. (1998), *Communities of Practice: Learning, Meaning and Identity*, Cambridge University Press

Winter, M. and Szczepanek, A. (2009), *Images of Projects*, Gower

Winter, M., Smith, C., Morris, P. W. G. and Cicmil, S. (2006), 'Directions for future research in project management: The main findings of a UK government-funded research network', *International Journal of Project Management* 24 (8)

Printed in Great Britain
by Amazon.co.uk, Ltd.,
Marston Gate.